Overexposed ...
(and slightly out of focus)

Overexposed ...
(and slightly out of focus)

One woman's adventures, misadventures, and an occasional misdemeanor ...

Bonnie L. Mack

iUniverse, Inc.
New York Lincoln Shanghai

Overexposed ... (and slightly out of focus)
One woman's adventures, misadventures, and an occasional misdemeanor ...

Copyright © 2006 by Bonnie L. Mack

All rights reserved. No part of this book may be used or reproduced by any means, graphic, electronic, or mechanical, including photocopying, recording, taping or by any information storage retrieval system without the written permission of the publisher except in the case of brief quotations embodied in critical articles and reviews.

iUniverse books may be ordered through booksellers or by contacting:

iUniverse
2021 Pine Lake Road, Suite 100
Lincoln, NE 68512
www.iuniverse.com
1-800-Authors (1-800-288-4677)

The views expressed in this work are solely those of the author and do not necessarily reflect the views of the publisher, and the publisher hereby disclaims any responsibility for them.

ISBN-13: 978-0-595-41754-4 (pbk)
ISBN-13: 978-0-595-86095-1 (ebk)
ISBN-10: 0-595-41754-X (pbk)
ISBN-10: 0-595-86095-8 (ebk)

Printed in the United States of America

Theo Rudman, who believed in me,
Ada Debevic for relentless encouragement,

also

Bill Poindexter and Shirley Trankle
(Always willing to venture to whatever crazy corner of the world I dragged them,
and without whom my travels would not have been as much fun.)

Contents

Preface.. *xi*

Chapter 1:   Close Calls & Other Experiences.......................1

Escaping by the skin of my ...

    A Woman's Nightmare ... a suitcase loaded with clothes, but nothing to wear! (Egypt)... 2

    A long night's journey into day ... (Cairo to Amman) 8

    I'll pass on the barbeque—just bring on the gauchos and sangria! (Buenos Aires).. 11

    Proof that a woman can stay the course! (Tunisia) 13

    Long drive through a small town ... (Tunisia)..................... 18

    An experience beyond my wildest imagination ... (China)........... 22

    Things don't necessarily get easier the second time around ... (China)... 23

    One last climb—for old time's sake! (China) 25

    "R&R" (rockin' and rollin') at the beach ... (Mombasa)............. 27

    A dining experience "down under" ... (Christchurch) 29

    Don't ever think you're lucky it didn't happen to you! (Okavango Delta).. 31

    Visiting headhunters was the easy part! (Borneo).................. 33

    Lucy (Ricardo) and Ethel (Merts) hit Hong Kong! (Hong Kong)........ 39

    Journey to the Netherworld (oops, I mean another world) ... (Myanmar)... 41

    If you've traveled enough, it has happened to you ... (Around the World).. 48

viii Overexposed ... (and slightly out of focus)

  Five little words ... "Remove your shoes—legs overboard!" (Baku National Park, Borneo). 51
  Hey, Ponce, go south—and inland! (Machu Picchu, Peru) 53
  The animals weren't the only ones that evolved! (Galapagos) 55
  Chairman Mao still has influence ... (Yangtze River). 57
  Apparently, Shangri-La is still elusive ... (Lhasa) 61
  Yakety yak—I don't think I'm goin' back! (Lhasa). 63
  "Mishap" is a title duly earned ... (Cabo San Lucas) 65

Chapter 2: Hotels, Lodges and Camps 69
The good, the bad, and the ugly!

  I felt like a princess—but I could have used a better "throne" ... (Cairo's Mena House). 70
  A quiet hotel in an inconspicuous border town—all was not what it seemed ... (Kiryat Shmona, Israel). 71
  Times passes, but some things never seem to change ... (Kiryat Shmona, Israel). 72
  Some things are better left to the imagination ... (New Winter Palace, Luxor, Egypt). 73
  Hotels for every taste—Tunisia offered it all (and much more) ... (Tunisia) 75
  A personal "Out of Africa" experience ... (Little Governor's Camp, Masai Mara, Kenya) 78
  Living like a maharajah ... (Sariska, India). 81
  Africa—a land of contrasts—and this is just the camps! (Botswana and Zimbabwe). 83
  Eleven years later ... I'm glad for the luxury! (Botswana and Zimbabwe). 85
  Camping out ... (Marrakech, Morocco). 88
  Watch out for "cozy" and "charming" ... (Das Cataratas Hotel, Iguassu Falls, Brazil). 90
  At last—a 5-star hotel! (Dubrovnik Palace Hotel, Dubrovnik, Croatia). 92

Chapter 3: Bathrooms 94
Can they really be called a "convenience?"

  Ladies, behind the aunt hill! (Africa) 95
  If your way is so great—stay with it! (China). 96

Chapter 4: Transportation 97
Getting there is half the fun!

Contents   ix

    If it's Tuesday, don't stop at red lights ... (Cairo)................98
    Dreams and fantasies really do come true ... (Kenya) 99
    Up, up and awaaaaay ... (Acapulco).........................102
    No three-ring circus, but a circus just the same ... (Jaipur).........103
    More experienced on elephants, we were ready for anything (well, almost) ... (Katmandu)......................................103
    Who needed a mahout—we were in charge now! (Chiang Rai) 104
    Home, home on the range ... (Kenya).........................106
    What has two wings and a small body? (Botswana)...............108
    The thrill of it all ... (Southern Africa) 110

Chapter 5:   Shopping 111
Woman's favorite sport!
    Maybe next time we should ask for grandma's false teeth? (Kashmir)...112
    How'd you do that? It was just a little magic ... (Kenya).........114
    Take home a souvenir from the past ... (Cairo)..................116
    Such a deal ... (Jerusalem) 119
    Sophia, you have competition! (Istanbul) 121
    Some women are suckers for men—me, I'm just a sucker for a bargain! (Bangkok)..124
    Strike one ... strike two ... no third strike for me! (Bangkok).........125
    So Carter discovered King Tut's tomb—I had my own discoveries ... (Bangkok)...126
    If you want it done right—find a woman! (Bangkok)...............128
    Two shirts, a watch, and thirteen bucks ... (Victoria Falls) 131

Chapter 6:   Weather 134
A traveler's best friend—or worst enemy!
    Beware of "light afternoon showers" ... (Acapulco) 135
    Pay more attention to those guidebooks—three strikes and you're out! (Acapulco)..136
    "Air-conditioning" had real meaning in Africa ... (Botswana)........138
    Who needs a sauna to help lose weight—evaporate it away! (Namibia)...139
    She huffed and she puffed, and she blew the plants down ... (Hong Kong)...140
    So, what's a little bit of rain? (Jakarta).........................142
    Pay attention to those weather reports ... (China).................144

Chapter 7:   Oh Those Men 146

From Ecuador to Egypt, Hong Kong to Croatia, and everywhere in between. As though the jetlag, strange food, and weather aren't enough to deal with ...

    It pays to dream big, because sometimes dreams really do come true! (Bogota). 147

    I dreamed of Fernando Lamas, but found myself in the arms of ... Pepe? (Quito). 149

    A perfect vacation, a perfect dinner, a perfect man (well, two out of three isn't bad)! (Hong Kong). 151

    Pursued like an Egyptian princess (hairy arms and all) ... (Egypt) 153

    Go for it the first time around ... (Split). 155

    The second time is never as good! (Split) 156

    Too good to be true ... (Mombasa) 158

    On a scale of one to ten, "Rangoon" was an eleven! (Yangon) 160

About the Author *161*

Preface

So ... I've been traveling around the world every year for more than three decades. What does that mean? It could mean that I'm either a travel agent, wealthy, or crazy. The responses are no, no, and definitely. I'm crazy about the world, all the fantastic places I've seen, the wonderful people I've met, and the incredible experiences that I'll never forget.

My parents introduced me to travel when I was still in diapers. By the time I graduated from high school, we had crossed the United States several times, visiting forty-six states, and journeying to parts of Canada and Mexico. Could anyone be surprised, when I spread my wings to more distant lands? Before long, everyone who knew me was asking where I was off to next. Would it be Morocco ... Japan ... the Middle East ... South America ... Africa? In order to make that determination, I'd sit on the floor and spread numerous travel brochures all around me. What a joy it was to have the whole world from which to choose.

Travel has challenged me in many ways. I'm not athletic, but I wasn't going to pass up the chance to climb the Great Wall (even if it was the third time). History wasn't one of my best subjects, and I never imagined I'd love exploring the ruins of Machu Picchu, Pompeii, or Ephesus. Extreme temperatures, humidity, and high altitudes aren't generally a traveler's best friends, but they've taught me to cope with things that are uncomfortable. I've learned to appreciate different cultures and architecture, and have become much more in tune, and at home, with the world around me. Long ago, I began to think of myself as an ambassador for America, whether at home or abroad. My life and work have been enriched, because when I cross paths with someone from another country, I can share my experiences and love of their country.

You may wonder why I have written this book ... hopefully, to entertain. If the reader is an experienced traveler, perhaps some of my tales will rekindle memories of their own experiences. And if the reader hasn't taken the opportunity to visit another country, I hope it will provide some encouragement to do so. The world is changing very quickly. I'm glad to have known it as it was, and I enjoy getting to know it all over again.

Chapter 1

Close Calls & Other Experiences

Escaping by the skin of my ...

Maybe you missed your plane ... or maybe you and your luggage were on *different* planes! Maybe danger was one step ahead of you, or one step behind you. Maybe that wonderful trip would have been a nightmare, if you'd been there at another point in time. Sometimes, close calls are exhilarating, and sometimes they make the hair on your head stand on end. If you've traveled very much, you've had your share of close calls, and they're the things you'll never forget. Then again, there are just some wonderful experiences you'll never forget, either.

A Woman's Nightmare ... A suitcase loaded with clothes, but nothing to wear!
Egypt 1976

One look at the lost luggage cage filled with hundreds of suitcases told me that anyone who left the airport with their bag was probably in the minority!

I was beginning to feel like the only woman who wore out her underwear from both sides. I'd wear it right side out during the day, and turn it inside out for the evening! Sometimes, by the time I retired, I was afraid it wouldn't be dry by early the next morning. Each night, I'd anchor my bra and panties to the table on my balcony with ashtrays, hoping that the same breeze that was aiding them in drying wouldn't blow them over the balcony, and down the Nile. *

Nothing makes a traveler's heart sink as quickly as a baggage conveyor belt with one last suitcase, and realizing it isn't yours! Having spent the last month before my departure sewing a new wardrobe for my three-week trip to the Middle East, my heart was lower than low. Could I really be surprised? After all, I'd made my way from Chicago to New York, Rome, Athens, and finally, Cairo. Grasping for anything that would raise my spirits, I reminded myself that at least my toiletries and cosmetics had arrived. Grateful I was for that, but after returning from the Cairo airport a second time empty-handed, I was becoming more doubtful than ever that my watermelon pink Samsonite suitcase would ever surface.

Perhaps one of the most frustrating moments was standing before the customer service representative, complaining that I'd been in the same clothes for three days. His eyes narrowed, as his nostrils flared. I could read his mind after taking one look at his djalaba, with signs of soil trailing down its front. He was probably thinking, "Three days! Three days! You complain because you've been wearing the same clothes for three days? I've been wearing mine for three weeks!"

After reminding him that it was the airlines' responsibility to provide us with some money to tide us over, he presented me with the equivalent of twenty-five U.S. dollars to go out and splurge on a new wardrobe.

I must admit that I did have a hint of hope the evening we arrived, when I saw the beautiful dresses and gowns on the Egyptian women attending a wedding at our hotel, the Meridian. The following morning, I informed our guide about what I'd seen, and asked him if he could take us shopping for some basic clothes. He was surprised at my question ... I was more surprised at his response. I raised my voice a few octaves.

"What do you mean there aren't any stores where we can buy some clothes?"

"Those women fly to Paris every six months to purchase their wardrobes." His calmness was annoying.

It was time to have a little talk with myself back in my room. I reasoned that I'd paid a lot of hard-earned money for this trip, and had anticipated it for a long time. I could either allow myself to be miserable, or I could make the most of it, resigning myself to the thought that somewhere in the Middle East, someone had probably taken my suitcase. It couldn't have been a mistake, because unlike black luggage, I had never seen another watermelon pink suitcase. If the new owner of my luggage had been successful in opening the locks, there was sure to be a big surprise. An array of brightly colored sundresses in an assortment of prints and flowers dominated my wardrobe—how utterly useless in a Muslim country.

After climbing inside the Great Pyramid and riding camels, my white pants were beginning to look off-white very fast. I quickly learned that Egyptian men are attracted to their camels like American cowboys are to their horses. About this time, my clothes were beginning to smell like the camels I had ridden, and the men trailed behind me everywhere I went, like flies.

To conserve my clothes, I stripped down whenever I was in my room for any period of time. Luckily, I was traveling alone, so I didn't have to worry about shocking a roommate. After glancing in the mirror from time to time, I decided to at least wrap a bath towel around myself, so I wouldn't be anymore depressed. One afternoon, I was sitting on my balcony in my towel writing post cards, as I watched the white-sailed feluccas gently floating down the Nile below me. I sensed that there was someone watching me, so I turned my head, only to find a man standing two floors above me, staring down at me. Thank goodness for the generous towel.

The following afternoon, I was delighted when my tour bus stopped at a huge souvenir store in the Grand Bazaar. At last, I found something else to wear—well, at least in the evening. It was a long tangerine-colored caftan, smartly decorated with embroidered trim down the front and on the sleeves. At dinner that evening, I was thankful to be wearing a fresh, new garment. The caftan allowed me to avoid wearing any underwear in the evening, so I could get it out to dry in plenty of time for its next use.

If I couldn't find anything to wear in Cairo, all hope of obtaining a wardrobe in Luxor was lost—that is, until our bus pulled up to the New Winter Palace Hotel, and I saw a kiosk near the driveway. What did I see blowing in the hot afternoon breeze? Caftans, lots and lots of caftans, long ones, short ones. I thought I died and went to heaven. I threw my cosmetic case in my room, and headed down to the kiosk, confident that I'd find something to wear.

"You buy caftan?" The young man smiled at me with a glint in his eye.

"Maybe."

"I make you a good price."

My attention was drawn to a colorful caftan with a border print. Actually, there were two borders, one of Nefertiti heads, and the other of camels. In both cases, the prints ran over the borders—not intentionally, I'm sure. But the green print would match my green earrings, and I might have found myself an ensemble after all. Stretching the sides of the caftan in front of me, I tried to guess if it would fit.

"Is there somewhere to try this on?"

"Yes, yes. You try on in my kiosk."

He pulled the clothes aside, and showed me a doorway. Apparently, he anticipated my hesitation.

"It's very private, no one will see you."

The afternoon temperatures in Luxor can rise to one hundred degrees or more in September, and the stale air in the kiosk made it difficult to breathe. I tugged and tugged, and fought to pull the long cotton garment over my head without destroying my hairdo. Finally, I made it. There was even a little room to spare. I stepped outside to take a glimpse in the full-length mirror that had some nasty cracks down the center.

"Beautiful. You look very beautiful," remarked the young salesman.

I was about to bargain for the price, when I noticed a shirt made of the same fabric and print. Ever practical, I reasoned that this would give me another option, because I could wear it with my dingy white pants. But again, I knew I'd have to try it on. I tugged the long caftan over my head, and was standing in my underwear, about to pull the shirt on, when suddenly the clothes that were hanging around me providing privacy had a parting of their ways, like the Red Sea. I clutched the shirt in front of me.

"What do you think you're doing?"

"It's no problem, I'm like a brother," the teenager offered a lame excuse.

"You're no brother! I don't have any brothers, and if you don't give me privacy right now, I won't buy anything from you."

Hastily, I finished trying on the shirt, put my clothes back on, and dashed out of the kiosk, as though being chased by a swarm of bees. We finished haggling about the price; I paid him, and was ready to walk away.

"You have smoke?"

"I don't smoke."

"Smoke, smoke," he gestured with his fingers, and a sly grin.

Then I realized that he had more in mind than a cigarette. I gathered up my clothes, and sprinted back to the safety of my hotel. I was elated that I had finally found something else to wear during the daytime, so I eagerly climbed into my new caftan, and headed down to the souvenir shop at the hotel.

"Look, Elsie, doesn't that girl look lovely in her caftan?" the chubby woman asked her elderly companion.

"Thank you, but you wouldn't think this was such a lovely caftan if it was the only thing you had to wear. The airlines lost my luggage."

"Well, dear, you look adorable anyway."

I might have looked pretty cute (sort of "dressed for the location"), but the heavy cotton garment was like wearing lead in the desert heat, as we explored Queen Hatshepsut's tomb in the Valley of the Queens the following day. The tour guide was expounding on the queen's accomplishments, as I tried to find the only bit of shade around, and began fanning myself with my caftan.

"Hot, isn't it?" One of the ladies on my tour commented.

"It's even hotter in this heavy cotton caftan."

"Well, honey, you're young, you have good legs, lift it up! That's what I'd do if I were your age."

Dare I? I lifted it to mid-calf.

"Higher" she encouraged me.

By the time it was just above my knees, a breeze engulfed me—ahhhh!

As our plane approached the runway in Aswan the following day, I noticed that it appeared to be a good-size city. Marie, one of the ladies on my tour, was also without her luggage. Following our arrival at the beautiful

Oberoi Hotel, we decided to take the complimentary ferry from our island hotel to the mainland, in search of some clothes.

As everyone is aware, the French and English have left remnants of their colonial past in Egypt. It was obvious that their influence was still prevalent, because tourists from both countries frequent Egypt for its warmth and sunshine. Making our way through one dark, dusty store after another, we were dismayed to see that the only "clothes" available came in the form of French bikinis. One look at them, and I realized that my pre-teen training bra had more fabric than both pieces of these bikinis—so much for any clothes.

We were very discouraged, when we arrived back at the hotel—empty-handed once again. The afternoon heat was almost debilitating, and the swimming pool looked so inviting, if only I could find something to wear. I made one final trip to the hotel's souvenir shop, and noticed several bolts of Egyptian cotton fabric. I turned to the shopkeeper.

"If I buy some fabric, may I borrow your scissors for a half hour?"

He was puzzled by my intentions, but reluctantly agreed. Though I selected the same pattern as on the caftan and the shirt I acquired in Luxor, I purchased it in another color—you know, to give my new wardrobe some diversity.

"As I recall, you said that you sew, but what are you going to do with this fabric? You don't have a sewing machine," Marie had a quizzical expression on her face.

"You'll see."

She followed me back to my room, and watched as I cut a double triangle connected in the middle, then a rectangle and, finally, a narrow strip of cloth.

"A bathing suit!"

"Let's hope it works," I picked up the pieces and headed for the bathroom. Minutes later, I returned to the bedroom.

"You look adorable; I wish I had your figure!" Marie was encouraging. "But how did you put it together?"

I explained that I folded the bottom like a diaper, tied the sides, and tucked in the ragged edges. The rectangle served as the top, and the narrow strings tied it in the center and around my neck, like a halter. Now, for the real test ... down to the pool. Carefully, I slipped the matching shirt over my head, so I could walk through the hotel lobby with some sense of modesty.

Fortunately, the pool area wasn't too crowded, because as I lifted the shirt gently over my head, one of my ample "endowments" peeked from beneath the halter-top. Hastily, I tucked my appendage back where it belonged, and tried to compose myself. I walked tentatively to the edge of the pool, and gently slipped into the cool water. Clearly, this was not a suit for swimming, but it served me well for just standing in the refreshing water.

On the flight back to Cairo, I glanced down at my lap. There sat a plastic bag with big black printing, *Meridian Hotel Cairo ... Laundry.* Inside what had become my luggage were two caftans, one shirt, and my "bathing suit." It was comforting to know that this time, when I arrived in Cairo, my clothes would be there with me.

*Published as a sidebar in *the thong also rises,* Traveler's Tales 2005

A LONG NIGHT'S JOURNEY INTO DAY ...
CAIRO TO AMMAN 1976

I don't know which part of the "journey" had the least appeal, flying to Damascus, and driving through the country in the middle of the night by bus, or the mere fact that the Syrians were even less enamored with Americans in 1976.

"The good news is that we'll have another day here in Cairo at the beautiful Mena House Hotel, to enjoy the swimming pool and gardens—perhaps spending the day relaxing, for our evening flight to Jordan."

Who was he trying to kid? Giovanni, our Italian tour guide, tried to put a positive spin on yet another Egypt Air blunder. Looking around his little "family" of tourists with trepidation, he added, "We'll be met in Damascus by someone who will accompany us on our bus journey across the border." Damascus? Bus? It was all suddenly clear, and the bad news was beginning to outweigh the good—but I had no idea by how much at this point. There was much more in store for us, but little did we know that before the next forty-eight hours were over, we'd all feel like we were competing in a marathon.

The Egypt Air flight had barely lifted off the ground, when every male on the plane (or so it seemed), crowded the aisle to use the lavatories. With little effort, they managed to trash them in record time. Danny, a tour member about my age, saw me waiting for my turn.

"Are you sure you really want to go in there?" He asked.

"It's not a matter of 'wanting,' but needing."

"Well, it's pretty bad. Let me see what I can do before you use it," he kindly offered.

Apparently, he disposed of the paper towels that had lined the floor, because remnants of damp paper clung to the soles of my sandals. He flushed the toilet, and wiped off the seat and floor.

Finally, our plane touched down in Damascus. All the ladies in our group who weren't brave enough to use the lavatories on the plane headed for those in the airport. I was waiting outside, when an elderly women came rushing around the corner, her face flushed.

"What's wrong, Doris?" I asked. She looked like an armed guard had interrogated her.

"I walked into the washroom and there was a man in there—going to the bathroom!"

I reminded her that this was customary in the men's room, as I pointed to the caricature of a man's head on the door. It must have been around midnight, but Doris was now wide-eyed *and* wide-awake. A bus transported us from the airport to a hotel in downtown Damascus, where we met our escort. Simply requiring one just to drive through the country added to the mystery and tension, making us feel like we were characters straight out of an adventure novel.

The swaying of the bus soon put me to sleep. Somewhere along the way, we stopped at the border, because I remember being awakened to hand over my passport. Through heavy eyelids, I peeked out the window and noticed that dawn had just broken. There were some marvelous Roman ruins that appeared to be part of an amphitheater. Ordinarily, I'd be disappointed that we didn't have time to explore the ruins, but not now. I raised my arm, passport in hand, and soon fell fast asleep again.

At 6:45 AM, our tired bus crept up the driveway to our hotel, the Intercontinental Amman.

"Okay, everyone," Giovanni announced, "here's the schedule. Those who have signed up for the optional tour to Petra, we'll be leaving at 7:15, so that gives you a half hour to get to your room, change clothes, if you need to, grab a quick breakfast, and meet in the lobby."

Was this man serious? We had just traveled through the night, and now we had several hours ahead of us in a car? Like it or not, at 7:15 AM we packed ourselves into the car, like pickles in a jar, and began our drive for several hours through the desert to the city of the Queen of Sheba. At last, we arrived, and began straightening our limbs, as we rolled out of the car.

"You'll be riding through the canyon on horseback," the local guide announced.

Horseback? Did he say, "horseback?" Maybe I didn't read the optional tour flyer closely, because I'm sure the word "horseback" would have caught my attention. It's not that I don't like horses, but we don't seem to see things in the same perspective. I want to go left; they want to go right. I want to move ahead; they want to stay put. And I won't even mention that our timing is always off—I'm up when they're down, then we come crashing together, as I bounce along like a sack of potatoes. I'm much better on a camel—but that wasn't even an option.

My horse and I lumbered along the shadow of the steep canyon walls. It was almost like winding through a crevice, because the path between the rocks seemed so narrow. In the far distance, I could catch a glimpse of the most beautiful edifice, and what looked like elaborate pillars on the front of an ancient building stood before me. With the hot morning sun glaring down on us, the building gave the illusion of being on fire. The contrast of the deep blue sky overhead made me gasp at the beauty before me. The most surprising thing was that the structure was carved *into* the rocks, rather than freestanding. We dismounted our horses, climbed the stairs, and passed through the entrance to what was known as the "Treasury." The ceiling looked like multi-colored marble—gold, brown, and russet, with purple veins—but it was actually the beautiful natural colors of the rocks. The entire city was carved into the mountainside, and resembled the false fronts used in Hollywood movie sets to depict a street scene. We proceeded on horseback throughout the city, in awe of the craftsmanship that withstood many centuries.

After a full day of traveling and sightseeing, we returned to our hotel in Amman. It was 7:00 PM, and we had no opportunity to clean up before dinner. Gazing around me, I couldn't help but chuckle. We all looked like snowmen, because everyone's hair (not to mention their clothes) was covered in layers of white powder from the dusty desert paths taken by our horses.

Bedtime couldn't come fast enough, and I was glad I didn't have a roommate with whom to share the bathroom. I quickly showered and took what seemed like another nap before it was time to get up and continue our journey to Israel.

Exhausting as it was, our marathon from Egypt to Petra by plane, bus, car, and horse was one I knew I'd never forget. To enforce the memory, I had been home only a few weeks, when my mother was reading the newspaper headlines.

"Did you to go Amman, Jordan?" she asked.

"Yes, why?"

"Where did you stay?"

"We were at the Intercontinental Amman, why?"

"It seems that terrorists stormed the lobby with machine guns, killing everyone in sight, including the hotel personnel."

At times like this, you *don't* tell your mother that your room was just a few yards off the lobby.

I'LL PASS ON THE BARBEQUE—JUST BRING ON THE GAUCHOS AND SANGRIA!
Buenos Aires, Argentina

"Tomorrow we'll be driving to the pampas, where we'll have a real Argentinean barbecue. Afterwards, we'll be entertained by the gauchos, Argentina's version of the cowboy. And for those of you who are interested, there will be a chance to go horseback riding."

WOA! That last comment about the horseback riding (spoken by our guide Paul) really got my attention. All horses seem to know they definitely hold the reins on me. I'm at their mercy.

When my friend Geri and I awoke the morning of the "big event," we were less than enthused, because it was raining outside. The best we could hope for was that the barbecue would be moved indoors. By the time we arrived at the pampas area outside Buenos Aires, we were sorry we had come. It rained all the way there, and we could feel the dampness through to our bones. Fortunately, the ranch's proprietor moved the barbecue to a pavilion, where he stapled plastic around the open windows, to keep the rain out. No, this was not going to be one of the better days on our tour.

We took our places at picnic benches inside the pavilion, and the staff immediately placed a pitcher of sangria on each table. Well, maybe it would help to take away the chill. By the time we finished our pitcher, we were warming up quite nicely. One of the Japanese men in our group walked over to the table, pitcher of sangria in hand. "Would you like our pitcher? We don't drink wine," he said as he offered it to us. Not wanting to be rude, we thanked him, and filled our glasses yet again.

Steaks, sausages, potatoes—we heaped the food onto our plates, and ate like we hadn't seen food in a week. We were still chewing the last few mouthfuls, when the entertainment began. The gauchos took their places in the center of the pavilion, and began stomping their boots, and waving their lariats overhead, as they danced their little hearts out. The music was getting louder, and before I knew what was happening, one of the gauchos came over to me, took my hand, and ushered me to the center of the floor. Putting his arm around my waist, he kicked his heels, and spun me around like a top. I don't know if it was all those ballet lessons I had as a little girl, or the sangria (most likely, the sangria), but I followed his footwork like a shadow. He jumped, I jumped; he twirled, I twirled, he dipped me, and I followed his lead, and leaned backwards. Applause! Applause!

The next thing I knew, our guide was clicking the heels of *his* shoes, jumping around the dance floor and—what was he doing? It looked like break-dancing. Paul was spinning around on the ground (in his nice leather coat), like a saucer on end. More applause! We were so busy dancing and singing, that no one missed not being able to go horseback riding (least of all, me).

The ride back to Buenos Aires was a long and very quiet one. I sat on the arm of my seat, and looked at the sea of bobbing heads all around me. Except for me, everyone in the group was sleeping. Never would I have thought that a day that promised to be a disaster from the start, would end up so much fun.

PROOF THAT A WOMAN CAN STAY THE COURSE!
TUNISIA

There was an urgent knock at the door of my hotel room. "It's Chris, open the door," he said sternly. When I did so, he brushed past me and crossed to the other side of the room, in a determined manner. "We have to talk," he began. "About what?" "About the trip. I think it might be better if you stayed in Tunis." "What are you saying? I'm supposed to spend the rest of the trip in Tunis—here at the Meridian Hotel—while you go off by yourself?"

"Why, after all the time we spent planning this trip, are you making such a suggestion?" I was shocked and puzzled.

"I'm just not sure you can cope with what we might encounter," he responded.

I was livid—how dare he suggest such a thing! "When did you come up with this idea?" I shouted. But before he could answer, I blurted, "I have no intention of staying in Tunis by *myself*! We planned this trip together for a year, and we're going to take it together—and you needn't be concerned about how I can cope with things!" End of conversation ... exit Chris.

I was raring to go the next morning. We checked out of the hotel, and were on the highway out of Tunis in a relatively short time. All of a sudden, our rental car coughed and choked, and died. No matter how hard he tried, Chris couldn't get it started again. We stood in the hot sun, just looking at our dead car, when a man walked up to us from across the highway, where there were some houses scattered over the dusty rural landscape. The middle-aged man was dressed in a white shirt, trousers, and a wool jacket—and it was already very hot. He rolled up his sleeves, lifted the hood of the car, and started playing with the wires and spark plugs. After what seemed like a long time without much success, he slammed the hood down.

Chris turned to me, "Someone will have to go back to Tunis to get help."

By this time, I could read his mind, and had a funny feeling about who that someone was. "Why can't we both go?" I pleaded.

"Because we have all our things in the car, so one of us has to stay here. You'll have to go back to the rental car company," he said very seriously.

I knew it! I'd already distinguished which someone was doing what. "Why me?" I asked.

"I'm not sure it would be safe for you to be left here alone" he answered.

Was this man crazy? And just how did he think I was going to get back to Tunis? I was in luck after all; the man's young son, who appeared earlier, led me down the road a short distance to a bus stop, and told me where to get off in the city. I would have felt safer locked inside the car in the heat, than cramped in a bus full of local people staring at me.

It couldn't have been more than a few hours since we checked out of the Meridian Hotel, when I found myself back there again. I dashed across the lobby, looking frantic, and stopped at the registration desk. The young man was shocked to see me, while I was glad to see a familiar face.

"What are you doing here? What happened?" he asked. After I relayed our predicament, he phoned the rental car agency for me, and gave the taxi driver directions on where to take me.

"No problem," the man at the Avis desk responded, after hearing about our plight. "I'll send our mechanic back with you in another rental car."

"But what if he can't fix the other car?" I asked in concern for the mechanic.

"Well, he'll sleep in it over night, and make his way back to Tunis for help—not to worry."

Sometime later, I found myself in another rental car, sitting beside a young man who couldn't speak English. This was, indeed, going to be a challenge, because I couldn't tell him where we left our car. I only knew where we were headed, and that we were on the highway. Then I began to worry—what if we were on the wrong road back to the car? What if I couldn't find Chris? What would I do all alone in Tunisia?

Finally, I began recognizing land formations. Not long afterwards, I found our car—but where was Chris? Fear rose inside me. He had insisted that someone needed to stay with the car, because our luggage was inside, and here it was, abandoned. Had something happened to him? Was he kidnapped or robbed? I heard my name being called, and looked across the road to see Chris dashing over the dry, dusty ground towards me with a big smile on his face.

"I thought you were going to stay with the car—where have you been?" I asked.

"Don't worry, I could keep an eye on the car from that house over there. The man invited me back to his house, where he insisted that I have something to eat ..." Then he rambled on about their conversation.

"How do you know all this? You don't even speak the same language!" I blurted out.

"We may not speak the same language, but that doesn't mean we didn't understand each other" he said defensively.

By this time my blood was starting to boil. Here I was, frantically making my way back to the city—and much worse, trying to find my way back to Chris, when I wasn't certain where I'd left him in the first place—and he was lunching and chumming it up with the guys!

We'd lost enough time already, so there was no point in arguing. We bade farewell to the mechanic from Avis, and continued down the highway in our new car. After several hours, it began to get dark, so we turned on our car lights. Then we noticed all the other cars didn't use their lights; and when they saw ours, they flashed their bright lights, urging us to turn ours off. It wasn't bad enough that we didn't know *where* we were going, now we couldn't see where we were going and, more importantly, we couldn't see any of the other cars driving through the open stretches in the blackness of the Tunisian night.

At last, we found ourselves in the little town of Le Kef, overlooking the Algerian border. It was pretty late, and the streets were empty. Chris managed to find a place to park, and turned to me.

"That looks like a hotel across the street, you'll have to see if they have any rooms."

Why was I always being given an assignment to perform?

Not many American tourists visit Tunisia, which is one reason we found it so appealing. However, I don't think we realized the problem we would have communicating with the local people outside of Tunis. Most of the tourists hailed from France, and the Tunisians could easily converse with them. With much trepidation, I walked into the tiny hotel's lobby and prepared to use sign language to ask for two rooms. Good fortune was on my side again, because the proprietor understood English, and gladly took me to see the rooms he had available. I peeked inside the door to the first room, and felt as though I was stepping inside someone's attic; the second room looked about as appealing. But they were clean, and we were tired. Minutes later, I walked outside to tell Chris I'd found us two rooms. Throwing his arms around me, he bent down to give me a big hug.

"Good girl ... I knew you could handle it," he said with a wide smile. Somehow, I felt as though I'd passed another test. How many more would there be, before Chris was convinced that I could handle whatever came our way? Little did I know ...

Before leaving home, I had a crash course in driving a stick shift. A friend was kind enough to volunteer the use of her car, and we headed off everyday at lunchtime to a hotel parking lot near our office. One day, I peered above the steering wheel to find a security guard standing in my way. He startled me, and I slammed on the brakes.

"Miss, I'm the hotel's security guard, and I've been watching you driving around the parking lot over and over again. May I ask what you're doing? You keep passing up all the available parking spaces."

I explained that I was learning to drive a stick shift, and he just turned and walked away with a puzzled expression on his face. I was surprised that he didn't warn me not to return, but I wasn't certain that he believed what I told him.

When we planned the trip, Chris talked me into renting a car with a stick shift, assuring me that it wasn't difficult to drive. My "lessons" were only a means of introducing me to the principles of driving a stick shift, because Chris had experience with such things—or so he implied. After our parking encounter in Tunis, when *he* couldn't parallel park, and had a temper tantrum, I began to realize that his "experience" was as historic as some of the Roman ruins we were encountering. One day, he announced that it was my turn to drive—just when I thought he was doing so well, that I hoped he'd forget I had no experience.

"You can do it, there's nothing to it." He tried to sound encouraging.

Of course, I had no problem on the open highway, but driving through the little towns made me nervous. On one occasion, I was trying to back out of a parking spot across from an ancient Roman coliseum, when I turned around to find that some camels appeared out of nowhere, and were lingering behind the car, causing me to slam on the breaks and lean on the horn. Camels darted hither and yon, and angry owners shook their fists at me.

In the next few days, we explored sacred religious cities, more historic sites, and Roman ruins. We'd stay at a deluxe resort hotel on the edge of an oasis, ride camels through the palm groves in the desert, cross the great "Chott el Djerid" salt flats (where the movie *Star Wars* was filmed), and spend the night in a cave "hotel." Oh yes, and in between, we were on the verge of finding ourselves in jail. But I managed to stay the course. Each day was a new adventure—some good, and some not so good. It wasn't until a few years later, when I met Chris's mother that she told me how she informed her son that he was very lucky to have had such a good companion to get through so many potentially serious experiences. Now I was even more proud that I stood my ground, and stayed the course.

LONG DRIVE THROUGH A SMALL TOWN ...
TUNISIA

Unlike the previous days, our car didn't break down, and there weren't any dangerous salt flats to cross. All in all, we'd had a pretty leisurely drive.

Only minutes before, the tiny Tunisian village had been void of inhabitants, a ghost town. It was mid-afternoon, and the sun burned its way through every living creature, so that anyone with an ounce of sense was indoors. There were few cars beside ours on the dusty main street that separated one side of the village from the other. My last words still rung in my ears, "Oh my god, oh my god" I shouted, turning to my companion Chris with horror in my eyes. He slammed on the brakes and looked at me, his eyes drawn to mine like a magnet. They reflected the same disbelief. Before we even knew what he hit, Arab men appeared from every nook and cranny. Like flies around a ripe, red watermelon, they swarmed around the car, peering at us from behind black beards and mustaches. Our hearts sank, as one of the men lifted a young boy from the dirt road and brushed him off, and then he raised the twisted bicycle to an upright position.

Word travels fast in a small town—particularly *bad* word—and before we could get our composure, a policeman pushed his way through the crowd. Bending down, he looked into the car at the two of us, seemingly glued to the seat. "Park there ... follow me," he said in English heavily burdened by a thick accent. Turning away, he walked towards a stone building that served as the police station. By the time we entered, the child was waiting inside with an old man. After the policeman spoke to the youngster in Arabic, a tear trickled down the child's dirty cheek. It was then that we noticed he was cross-eyed.

Having been ill the night before, I was in dire need of a bathroom. "Toilet?" I asked. The policemen pointed to a door. Opening it, I found myself peering into an outside courtyard. On the far side, two dirty men, whom I assumed were prisoners, were crouched against the stone wall, savoring the little bit of shade provided by a tree on the other side. I looked at them. They looked at me, rubbing their eyes. They must have thought they'd been sitting in the day's heat too long, when I entered the courtyard, my red hair aflame in the sunshine, and my sundress billowing in the hot breeze. My eyes darted around the otherwise empty area, and I noticed a wooden shack that I presumed was "*le toilette*." Feigning confidence, I sprinted to the shack, and locked myself in. I still couldn't come to terms with how quickly our leisurely drive through a sleepy town was turning into a nightmare.

When I returned, Chris informed me that we were to drive the boy and his grandfather to the next town, where the police chief was more fluent in English. To our surprise, the policeman reacted kindly towards Chris and myself; whereas, the boy was in tears after his questioning. Now we were being asked to drive the "victim" to another town?

In these small towns, it wasn't difficult to find the police station, particularly with the chief waiting for us on the step. The boy shuffled over to him and mumbled a response to an apparent inquiry. Again, the policeman grumbled back and, as usual, the tears started to trickle. "We will take him to the doctor," the chief informed us, while opening the door of his police car. Police chief, little boy, grandpa, Chris, and myself—we all piled into the hot vehicle. The ride was short, but there was ample time for some frightening thoughts to race through my mind, What if they wanted to put us in jail? Could I be considered guilty, if Chris was the one driving? I looked all around me for a hotel, in the event that he was arrested, and I had to stay in town for a trial—they *did* have trials in Tunisia, didn't they? We pulled up to a bright pink house. It reminded me of a big bottle of Pepto-Bismol, but I realized that the vision was more of a mirage, after having spent half the previous night in my hotel's bathroom.

The elderly doctor opened the door, and invited us in. Was I hallucinating, or was that a huge metal Eiffel Tower standing on the fireplace mantle? I assumed that it was a souvenir from a trip to Paris. Collecting my thoughts, and refocusing on the subject at hand, the little boy finished relating his story for still a third time, and the doctor's response initiated the tears once more. Chris paid him the equivalent of about two dollars and fifty cents, and we were off to the hospital. Hospital? I had visions of MRIs, CTs, the usual assortment of x-rays, and a big bill. "Rich Americans," I thought to myself, "that's what they all think, isn't it?"

At the small hospital, Chris, the chief, and I made ourselves as comfortable as one could be on a hard bench, while someone whisked the boy and grandpa into another room. I glanced at the dingy green walls in the corridor, and began to wonder if the hospital even had an x-ray machine. A few minutes later, the boy returned, rubbing his behind. It was obvious that he'd been given a shot. The interesting thing was that no one even bothered to look at his knee, the cause for his apparent limp. The skin wasn't broken, but neither had it been washed for an examination.

Back at the police station, the chief informed us that we were free to go. As quickly as they arrived, our apprehensions waned.

"How will they get back to their village?" Chris asked the chief.

"They'll take the bus."

"No, we'll be happy to drive them back."

Pulling Chris aside, I suggested that maybe I should wait at the police station, "you know, so no one gets the idea that we're *anxious* to get out of here." Agreeing that it wasn't a bad idea, Chris suggested that perhaps I could wait for him there, since I hadn't been feeling well. The chief was only too agreeable. Little did I know that while one adventure had just concluded, another was about to begin. Leading me to his office, the chief offered me a chair.

"Would you like something to drink?"

"Do you have a Coke?"

He left the room, and returned with a cold bottle and a big smile, as he handed it to me. "We don't see many women from the outside coming to our little town."

"Outside?" He made me feel like I was from another planet. Now it was my turn to smile.

"How old are you?" He pressed on, making me nervous at his first attempt to converse. He was a little too direct for my comfort.

"I'm thirty-two," I said, trying to fake a smile.

"How old do you think *I* am?"

I kept telling myself to be diplomatic. I wanted to say that he looked forty-five, but I reasoned that even if that was a complimentary response, I really needed to dig deeper for a more flattering one.

"It's hard to tell," I tried to fudge. But I knew that answer wasn't going to suffice. "I'd guess about thirty-four."

"I'm twenty-eight." With that announcement, he proudly puffed up his chest. I was happy that I'd lied about how old I thought he was. I only wished it had been a bigger lie, but he didn't seem offended. I was becoming increasingly uncomfortable, with all the personal questions, when he pressed on again.

"Are you married?"

Oh my goodness, what should I say? He knew Chris and I were traveling together, but he didn't know it was only as friends. If I said yes, and for some reason he had to see our passports, or was able to determine that I lied, he might think we were hiding something. And if I said no, he might get the wrong impression about me. I decided honesty was the best resort.

"No," I muttered, after what seemed to me like a long hesitation.

"I'm not married either," he immediately perked up.

By this time I was really getting anxious. Where on earth was Chris? Had he somehow gotten lost on his return? With only one main road between towns, that wasn't likely. Maybe he had a flat tire. My mother always wanted a son-in-law, but I couldn't fathom calling her to tell her I'd be living in a one-horse Tunisian village as the wife of the Police Chief. *

"Would you like some lunch?"

"Thank you, but I'm not feeling well, so I don't think that would be a good idea." Didn't this guy ever give up? How much longer could I hold him off? My perspiration and shakiness only served to convince him that I was ill. Little did he know that it wasn't the result of any illness the night before.

Suddenly, Chris burst through the door. I couldn't hold back any longer, I dashed over to him and gave him a hug as though he was Lazarus rising from the dead.

"I was so worried about you."

"Oh, I'm fine. It's just that the drive was a little longer than I remembered. I gave the boy some money to have his bike fixed, and he seemed really happy."

By this time, I'd had enough of men, and was more than ready to be on our way, when Chris turned to the chief.

"I suppose we'd better have something to eat before we resume our journey. Would you like to join us?"

*Published as a sidebar in <u>*the thong also rises*</u>, Traveler's Tales 2005

AN EXPERIENCE BEYOND MY WILDEST IMAGINATION ...
CHINA 1987

It wasn't too many years after President Nixon "opened" the door to China with his visit, and our visit was pretty eye opening. To this day, China never ceases to amaze me.

We left our Beijing hotel early in the morning, because the drive to the Great Wall took hours ... hours being jostled around in our old tour bus, dodging thousands of Chinese people on their bicycles, pedaling furiously across the city to their places of work. Some had dead chickens dangling from the handlebars; others had bales of straw several feet high heaped on the back fender—how they managed to balance the load, which nearly dragged on the city streets, I'll never know.

Geri and I were lucky to have the front seats on the bus. Well, perhaps "lucky" wasn't the word for it, because when I wasn't filming through the front window, I was gasping at the dangerous antics of our driver. Using the brake wasn't an option, nor was using a directional signal. His method of announcing our oncoming presence was the horn—and he blasted it all the way from the hotel to the Great Wall—TOOOOOOOT ... TOOT, TOOT ... TOOOOOOT, TOOT, TOOT. After awhile, we gave up on even wanting to see the surrounding sites, and city life.

At last, we arrived at our destination. Our guide pointed out the two options, "On this side, we have the easy walk; and on this side, the walk is much more difficult, but the scenery is also more beautiful."

"We have to take the difficult walk," Geri said, as she turned to me with a plea in her voice, "because we want the most scenic photos." Thus, we began our ascent.

Steep stairs, small stairs, and ramps—the wall was a combination of them all. Some stairs were so steep that I tried to film Geri as she was approaching me, and it looked as though she was climbing up on her knees. Just when we were getting used to the high stairs, there was a series of stairs only about two inches high, throwing our tempo and balance off. Once we mastered that, we found ourselves climbing up a ramp. It was very hard on the legs, and especially difficult with my 35mm camera and all the heavy lenses hanging from my shoulders.

"Maybe it would be easier climbing up backwards," I suggested, as I turned myself around. Grabbing the handrail, I found that it was, indeed, a lot easier on the legs—until I became too top-heavy with my camera gear, and leaned forward, nearly rolling down the ramp. Thank goodness for those handrails, or I'd have found myself back at our starting point.

It wasn't terribly crowded, and the local Chinese people we encountered were, for the most part wearing their usual drab gray "Chairman Mao" clothing—pants and a jacket with a Mandarin collar.

I thought I was going to expire, but I kept telling myself, "One foot in front of the other; put one foot in front of the other. One foot ..."

"Geri, haven't we seen enough? I mean, it's just more wall—we don't have to climb the whole thing."

"You'll thank me, when we reach the precipice," she responded.

"But no one will know we've reached it—except us—and I won't tell." I tried to persuade her, but to no avail.

"You'll thank me," she said, with the implication that the subject was closed. Considering Geri was eighteen years older than I was, embarrassment gripped me, and I knew that I had little choice.

We finally reached one of the farthest ramparts that few tourists walk beyond. Gasping for breath, Geri was elated.

"We're ... we're ... we're finally here!" After her exclamation, she dropped down on a rock, and tears were streaming from her dark eyes.

"What's wrong? Are you okay?" I was concerned that she was having a heart attack.

"No," she answered, somewhat in awe, "I'm just so happy I climbed this far." Then my eyes filled with tears, and Geri noticed them. "Now see, aren't you glad we climbed all the way?"

"You're mistaking my reaction—these are tears of pain!"

~ FAST FORWARD ~

THINGS DON'T NECESSARILY GET EASIER THE SECOND TIME AROUND ...
CHINA 2000

I kept chugging along, climbing higher and higher, farther and farther from the entrance gate. I was feeling pretty proud of myself about now.

With the new highways in China, the drive to the Great Wall from Beijing took only about a third of the time it had thirteen years before. I couldn't believe how China had turned around since my first visit. Modern high-rises and new apartment buildings were everywhere—spectacular architecture, scaffolding, and construction equipment dotted the skyline.

I was equally surprised to see how the area around the wall had improved as well. Little shops replaced the wooden kiosks selling souvenirs. A variety of quality goods were available, and a nice hotel had been built nearby.

The tour guide explained our options, "This way for the easy walk, and the other direction for the more difficult, but more photogenic walk." There was no decision on my part—it was the "easy" walk this time. Hmmm? It certainly was much more crowded thirteen years later. There were a lot of young people, clad in the latest fashions. Cute little teenage girls were managing to climb the wall in their three-inch platform shoes and mini skirts. Of course, they had many young men willing to assist them in their efforts. I walked, and climbed—steep stairs, shallow stairs, and ramps.

I had to keep looking down to watch where I was walking. When my breathing became too labored, I figured I was entitled to take a rest (the first of several to come). There were young people, old people, many local people, and many tourists. Watching them was as interesting as taking the "required" photos from the wall. No one could deny that the scenery was spectacular, as the wall rambled through mountain after mountain, after mountain, on and on and on. I kept chugging along, climbing higher and higher, farther and farther from the entrance gate. I was feeling pretty proud of myself about now. There was nothing easy about the "easy" side of the wall—it was *all* difficult—and to think that I was thirteen years older, well, I was due for a good pat on the back.

Then I saw her ... one of the women on my tour was coming down the wall, on her way back to the bus. "You're on your way back already?" I asked, trying to imply that I was enjoying my "leisurely stroll" up the wall, taking photos along the way. I couldn't believe she had made it to the top ahead of me; why, she was several years older than myself, and she had knee surgery after she climbed waterfalls in Jamaica—five times!

~ FAST FORWARD ~

ONE LAST CLIMB—FOR OLD TIME'S SAKE!
CHINA 2005

I didn't know if I'd make it back to China a fourth time, so I steadied myself for one more climb. The scenery was as magnificent as I remembered, and I could soak my tired bones back at the hotel.

The super highway was faster—there were hardly any people on bikes anymore. Instead, they drove cute little motor scooters. Beijing was still building, and our hotel was fabulous. Green lawns and well-manicured parks dotted the landscape—even underneath all those highways! There were flowerbeds, bushes, and trees everywhere. China moved even faster in the five years since my last trip.

The guide pointed his finger at the wall, I felt like shouting, "I know, I know, this way for the easy climb, but the more photogenic walk is on the other side!" Okay, so let's see if I can make it as far on the "easy" side as I did five years ago. One foot in front of the other, in front of the other, in front of the other. On and on I climbed ... steep stairs, shallow stairs, and ramps. I allowed myself a rest break after a substantial walk, and immediately, found two giggly Chinese girls crowding in on me. One of them showed me her camera, and the other put her arm around me, smiling as her friend took our picture. Oh, yes, I'd forgotten, Westerners were still something of an oddity, despite what I thought were so many of us, compared to eighteen years ago. Then again, with such a large Chinese population, I guess we were somewhat sparse after all. I motioned to one of the girls to take my picture with the beautiful scenery in the background. Immediately, her friend put her arm around my shoulder, and gave a toothy smile for my camera.

I kept looking blocks ahead, and wondered if I could make it to the same destination I'd reached the last time. "Don't think about it," I told myself, "just keep walking—don't think about it." I huffed, and I puffed, and I ploughed on, and on, and on. Finally, I saw the camel stand, where one can pay to have their photo taken in a period costume sitting on a camel. I made it—I reached my destination! I was so pleased with myself. I really wasn't sure I could do it.

This moment needed a photograph. I turned around, and found a young, blond-haired, blue-eyed European man walking in my direction. I glanced around me—there weren't any smiling teenage girls, to impose themselves into my photograph. I approached the man, "May I ask you to take my photo?" "Of course," he said, taking my camera. Then, with a big smile, he handed it back to me, "Beautiful picture."

I felt satisfied. I'd done it—I'd climbed the Great Wall of China three times in eighteen years! I was feeling pretty proud of myself. Then I noticed an old lady nearing the top of the wall. POP ... hisssssss. I could hear my bubble bursting.

"R&R"(ROCKIN' AND ROLLIN') AT THE BEACH ...
Mombasa, Kenya

This was no "Beach Blanket Bingo" with Frankie and Annette on a beach in California. It was near suicide in Mombasa!

The waves threw themselves mercilessly on the beach, leaving clumps of black seaweed as far as the eye could see. Exhausted from the long, dusty drive from Tsavo East, the Serena Beach Hotel was a welcome respite. The white Moorish-style hotel overlooked the Indian Ocean. Fuscia bougainvilleas draped themselves over dark wooden balconies—a nice contrast to the bright white buildings and blue, blue sky. The swimming pool was tempting, but the warm ocean waters—mmmm, they were a treat for us Midwesterners.

Slipping out of my sandals, I waded through the hot surf, as I remembered how rough the Indian Ocean was, and how treacherous the undertow could be. Karen and I were jumping the waves with glee, but each time we rode high above the ocean's floor, we could feel ourselves being pulled out to sea. The restless waters wore us out, with their relentless rockin' and rollin'. Making a concerted effort to break ourselves free, we were finally able to wade to the shore. But fast on my heels was one last wave—bam! Crunch! Swoop! It caught me by surprise, knocked me flat on my stomach, and hammered my knee into the hard sand—not once, but twice. The pain was excruciating, but I managed to raise myself to my feet, and tear myself away from the encroaching waves, lest they repeat their dastardly deed.

I made my way slowly to the top of the embankment, and limped all the way back to my room. After removing a pound of seaweed from my swimsuit, and cleaning up the bathroom floor and tub, I noticed my knee—it was bigger than Donald Trump's ego! I raised my swollen leg on a stack of pillows, and balanced a towel filled with ice on the ballooning mound that was once a slender knee. Eventually, the pain began to subside, and I wrapped my still swollen knee in an elastic bandage.

The good thing about a safari is that most of one's time is spent sitting, either in a vehicle or around a lodge. I was fine as long as I was sitting, but my leg would get stiff, so every time I had to get up and walk somewhere, my leg had to adjust itself all over again. About the time it loosened up, it was time to climb back into our vehicle. In one of the villages, I bought a carved walking cane for about six dollars—I didn't feel it was much help, but it added to the mystique.

Whenever we arrived at a lodge, the staff would all ask what happened to my knee, so I'd explain that I had an accident on the beach in Mombasa. "That's too bad," they all responded sadly.

"Well, not really," I answered with a smile, "it sounds a lot more adventurous to say I hurt my knee on a beach in Mombasa while on safari, than to say I tripped on a sidewalk at home!"

A DINING EXPERIENCE "DOWN UNDER" ...
CHRISTCHURCH, NEW ZEALAND

Whenever I've encountered a "Kiwi" (nickname for New Zealander) on my travels, I always found them to be the friendliest of all people. This is probably no more evident than when one visits them on their home turf. Many tour operators include a "home visit" with local people for dinner. It's just such a visit that I'll never forget.

Our tour guide divided us into small groups of four, and Shirley and I anxiously awaited our ride. Before long, an elderly man entered the hotel lobby, and introduced himself as Jim, our host for the evening. During the ride to his house, Jim had little to say, so I tried to engage him in some small talk, but to no avail. Shirley and I looked at each other, thinking him rude to ignore my questions and comments. This wasn't going to be a very friendly evening, if the host ignored us.

When we arrived, Jim's wife Mary welcomed us at the door, and invited us into their parlor, which was like a giant step back into the fifties. Instead of carpeting, they had black-and-white twelve-inch tiles on the floor, and two red vinyl chairs dominated the room. The odd thing was that the rest of the furnishings were somewhat fussy, with lace doilies on the Formica-topped tables. It resembled a spruced up diner! We talked for a while, and I asked how Jim and Mary became involved in the home visits.

"We've always enjoyed meeting people from other countries, and when we retired and couldn't afford to travel anymore, we thought this was a nice way to continue meeting people. The home visits are on a voluntary basis; however, one needs to be interviewed and approved by the sponsoring organization in order to participate. Yes, we must meet certain criteria. The company sends someone out to see your home, and look at your china and crystal, before you're accepted for home visits."

"Well then, does the company reimburse you for your dinner expenses?" I asked.

"Goodness, no. We pay for the dinners ourselves."

At last, dinner was ready, and Jim showed us to the dining room, which appeared to be a converted bedroom. Meanwhile, Mary was off to the kitchen. The table was beautifully set with flowers, a lovely lace tablecloth, china, and crystal. Minutes later, she appeared with a shrimp cocktail appetizer. When we were finished, she cleared the table, asking Jim to put the dinner plates down. He did so somewhat absentmindedly, and then left the room, closing the door behind him. The four of us in our little group were chatting, when suddenly I noticed something on one of the plates. What *was* it? We all looked at the black spot on Mary's plate. Finally, I recognized it as a dead fly.

"My god!" I exclaimed, barely able to control my laughter, "Mary will die, if she returns and sees that fly on her good china. And just imagine what 'the company' would say, after all the interviews they put her through—a dead fly!"

Trying to compose ourselves before Mary and Jim returned, we looked at each other quizzically. When I got myself together, I reached for the plate, flipped the fly onto the floor, and wiped the plate off with Mary's napkin. I'd finished just in time, when the door opened, and Mary burst in with a platter filled with lamb. Jim trailed behind her with the mashed potatoes and vegetables.

After dessert, we returned to the parlor for more conversation. Jim resembled a butler that we've all seen in the movies at one time or another—tall, thin, bald, very English, and seeming very absent-minded. Finally, Mary informed us that he was hard of hearing, which explained his lack of conversation on the ride to their home. After a lovely visit, we thanked Mary for the wonderful dinner, and climbed into Jim's car for the ride back to the hotel. The temperature had dropped, and the windows were steaming up. Jim cautiously backed out of the driveway; however, I became nervous, because he continued driving with foggy windows. He put on the wipers, but the windows still wouldn't clear. Meanwhile, Shirley and I were clutching each other in the back seat.

"Darn car," Jim finally mumbled. "Just bought it, and I still don't know where to find all the buttons." Great, we were at the mercy of a deaf old man with bad eyesight, who didn't know how to drive his new car!

With help from the good lord, Jim managed to find his way to our hotel. But we often wondered if he ever made it back home that night.

Don't _ever_ think you're lucky it didn't happen to you!
Okavango Delta, Botswana, 1992

I couldn't believe that someone as big as Karen could be so frightened of the small bugs and spiders we'd come across at camp. I'm no fan of them either, but one has to be reasonable. I mean, is it worth capsizing a boat?

We'd been in Botswana for a few days, and were elated to learn that we'd be taking our makoro to one of the other islands in the Okavango Delta for some exploration. Back in 1992, the makoros were narrow two-passenger boats carved from trees. Passengers would sit on the floor of the boat in what looked like a chair without legs—just imagine a seat and a back which were easily removed, as they weren't permanently affixed to the boat. The passenger in the back would have to straddle the chair in front, one leg on each side. The "poller" or individual who guides the boat through the winding streams of the Delta with a long pole, stands in the back—sort of Africa's version of a gondolier. For the most part, the water is shallow and clear, though the vegetation generally blocks a view of the bottom.

Approaching the island, our poller instructed us to climb overboard into the cold waters of the Delta.

"Climb into the water?" we shouted back at him. "But why?"

"The water is too shallow; we'll have to walk to the island, or the boat will get stuck."

I looked ahead ... between us, the water, and the island lay lots of sloppy black mud. Then I looked at my yellow canvas shoes, and began removing them—this was going to be *very* messy.

Once we got to the banks of the island—through the mud and carrying our shoes—each of us looked for somewhere to sit down and clean the mud off our feet. The tree stump served us well and, grabbing a handful of dry leaves, we attempted to wipe as much mud off as possible, before climbing back into our shoes or sandals.

Unfortunately, we didn't spot any wildlife hiding out on the island; however, wading through the water from the boat, and slipping and sliding through the mud were reminiscent of childhood antics—only this time, we wouldn't get scolded! Karen and I were tucked inside our makoro on the way back to camp, when she became quite excited, almost capsizing the boat.

"There's a leech on my leg—get it off, quick, get it off!" She shouted, waving her arms around, and nearly capsizing the small boat

The poller reached over and plucked the nasty little devil from her leg. Secretly, I thought to myself, "Glad it wasn't *my* leg!"

As always, I enjoyed the beautiful scenery on the way back to camp. Wet reeds occasionally slapped us in the face, as the Delta's channels became very narrow. The sun was shining brightly, and the sky was so very blue overhead. It was another beautiful day. Then I looked down at the heel of my shoe. What *was* that on my once yellow canvas shoe? It was something red—it looked like blood. Blood? Could I have cut my leg on something in the water? Nothing hurt. I turned my leg around carefully, and then I found the source of the blood—it was another leech—sucking its little heart out. "Stay calm," I told myself. "After all, you didn't feel any pain; you didn't even know he was there."

"Karen," I called out, "guess what's on my leg—a leech!"

"What are you going to do about it?" she asked.

"What *can* I do about it? I guess I'll just have to wait until we get back to camp. I can't stop the boat now that we're in the rapids."

About a half-hour later, our makoro pulled into the little cove near our camp. Spotting our guide, I called out, "Ieuan, I have a leech on my leg—can you have someone pull it off!" One of the pollers came to my rescue, grabbing the husky little leech between his fingers. He gave one hard tug, and the bloodsucker released itself, leaving two little pricks in my leg that lasted for weeks. The incident left me thinking that just because something happens to someone else, doesn't mean it won't happen to you.

Visiting Headhunters Was The Easy Part!
Borneo 1993

Bad guide, long drive, lousy accommodations, but this was one excursion I'd never forget!

Shirley, Bill and I waited anxiously in the lobby of the Kuching Hilton, about to begin our adventure in Borneo. A young man walked over to us and introduced himself. Donnie was his name, and he was to be our guide up the Skrang River to the longhouse of the Iban tribe—former headhunters.

"Are you staying one or two nights at the longhouse?" he asked. According to our itinerary, we were to have two nights, with a third night back at the Kuching Hilton. I was surprised that he wasn't aware of the arrangements. "Do you want two nights with the Ibans?" he pressed.

"Is there a difference in the price?" I asked, thinking it would mean additional money.

"No, same price."

My companions looked to me for a decision; neither seemed to have any preference. Some questions flashed to my mind, "Are you sure you want *two* nights in a longhouse? What will we do all day?"

"Well, how about one night at the longhouse, and two back in Kuching?"

"Fine," he curtly responded. Sizing him up, I figured this rustic stuff must have a real appeal for a young stocky, macho guy.

Trying to be friendly, I asked, "Do you like your job?"

"Not particularly," he shot back, setting the tone for our excursion.

We weren't on the road long, but Donnie hadn't said anything about where we were going, other than that we would be driving for five hours to the river, then we'd take a longboat for an hour to our destination. I tried to break the ice by asking him some questions, when he instructed us not to talk to him while he was driving—so much for an educational experience.

I guess Donnie was pretty tired after the silent drive, because he settled himself in the back of the long, narrow boat (hence, the name "longboat") and fell asleep across the seats. By this time, we were all appalled at his attitude, and Bill began making snide remarks about him. I tried to calm Bill down, afraid that Donnie might be sleeping with one ear on alert, and we were at his mercy in the jungle.

As we disembarked about an hour later, Donnie pointed to the island in the middle of the river, not very far away.

"That is called Pig Island," the first bit of information he imparted in over six hours.

"Any particular reason why?" I asked.

"Well, the pigs used to live under the longhouse, but the Ibans found that they caused disease, so they moved them to that nearby island."

There was a shack straight ahead of us, built on the customary stilts. The walls were nothing more than wooden slats. I wondered what they stored there. Donnie led us up the old wooden steps.

"This is the guest house, where you'll be staying," he announced, waiting for our reaction. For once, we were totally speechless. What they apparently stored there were the tourists! As we entered the "guest house," there was a wooden table to our left with some chairs and wooden benches scattered here and there. Looking through the wooden slats that stood for walls, we saw a shriveled old woman wearing only a sarong around her waist, totally bare from the waist up. She was intent on raking something, but we didn't know what, because trash was everywhere.

"Your sleeping quarters are to your right," Donnie pointed out.

Surely he was mistaken—it looked like a stable—one aisle, with an old linoleum floor (remember linoleum?), and flanked on either side by three stalls. The stalls were about eighteen inches off the floor, and each had a dirty mattress resting on it. The walls were about halfway to the ceiling, and a worn old drape dangled from a rope across the top of each stall, so it could be pulled for privacy. Bill volunteered to cover the mattresses with the sheets that were provided for each of us, and struggled to slide the limp pillows into their "clean" cases.

Somehow, I found my voice, "Where ... where (I stuttered) is the toilet?"

"Oh, the toilet and shower are down there," Donnie pointed to a wooden shack at ground level with two doors.

"I'll be back later to cook dinner," he said, and was off in a flash.

My nerve resurfaced, and I decided to explore the "bathroom" facilities, while Shirley and Bill retreated to the kitchen chairs, where a hot breeze would occasionally push its way through the narrow slats. Anything had to beat being out in the scorching midday sun and humidity. I returned to join them sometime later.

Close Calls & Other Experiences 35

"Well, at least the toilet flushes—and there's even paper!" I was groping for anything positive at this point. "And the floors in the toilet and shower are cement!" I happily proclaimed. They weren't impressed. "I took a shower!" I announced. They looked blankly at me. "There's even a wooden table to put your clothes and things on." They *still* weren't impressed. "It felt good to get clean," I pushed on, "although there were a few spiders here and there, so you have to be quick about it."

Finally, Shirley found her voice, "That does it—no shower for me tonight!" But it was so unbearably hot and sticky, that I found enough nerve to take a second shower that afternoon (spiders or no spiders), just to cool off. With ninety-six percent humidity and temperatures around a hundred degrees, one was just as wet, whether they were in the shower or not.

As usual, Bill regaled us with some funny stories, while we relaxed. Donnie returned to start dinner. We peered into the next room, at what was referred to as the "kitchen." I guess the slats served a purpose after all, because occasionally a hot breeze passed through there as well. Donnie began chopping up the vegetables and chicken, tossing all the body parts into a wok with the veggies. Sometime later, he walked over to the wooden table with a big bowl of rice, and another of cooked chicken and vegetables. Hesitating, we each took a modest serving. Wait a minute, this stuff was good, *really* good! Donnie may not be much of a tour guide, but he was one heck of a cook. We ate, and ate, and ate like there was no tomorrow, until every last morsel was gone. After all, we reasoned, what were all those shots we had before our departure for anyway, if not to protect us from getting sick?

That evening, after dinner, Donnie led us to the longhouse of the Iban tribe. As the name indicates, the house is a long wooden building on stilts. The tribe practices communal living, and the longhouse is divided into several private quarters. Each family has its own central room, kitchen, and upstairs (but the "stairs" consist of a long tree trunk with what would appear to be steps—each about half the size of a small plate). The stairs connect the first and second floors. A long corridor runs outside each of the private rooms. This is the community's common area, where the tribe gathers for meals and entertainment, sitting on straw mats. Women were sitting cross-legged working on their crafts, and numerous young children were running around playing, while music and dancing were contributing to the evening's entertainment. Think of the arrangement as a condominium of sorts, without any decorating regulations or restrictions. The common hallway is likened to a community recreation room, with a myriad of activities all going on at once. Perhaps the most noticeable difference is that the Ibans have a huge net hanging overhead, suspending the skulls of their enemies. One must keep in mind, however, that only the heads of enemies were hunted ... although there were many occasions for hunting, such as to celebrate a new baby or engagement, or to impress a future wife, etc.

Shirley and I held plastic bags with gifts in our laps as we signed in the guest book. It's customary for guests to bring the chief gifts for his tribe. Of course, the chief prefers liquor and cigarettes, but we refused to contribute to alcoholism and cancer, so instead we brought things for the children, like bright-colored sunglasses and beach balls imprinted with the globe. Our old costume jewelry was a big hit in Zimbabwe, so we cleaned out our drawers, and brought the bangles along as gifts. Sitting nervously, we could only hope we wouldn't become the Chief's enemies. Bill, meanwhile, was handing out mini Swiss army knives, and demonstrating their uses. We thought that a bad choice for gifts to headhunters, but he was proud of his idea.

The young Chief looked a little disappointed at the absence of liquor and cigarettes, but seemed satisfied enough when he saw the children's pleasure with their gifts. They were beautiful children, and it was difficult not to burst out laughing as they ran around with lime-green sunglasses perched upside down on their little noses. I was surprised to recognize one of my old necklaces dangling from the neck of a five-year-old boy. The boys were most impressed by the jewelry, while the sunglasses were a hit with the little girls. An old man motioned for me to come over. He held a large coin earring with a profile of Julius Caesar in his hand. Since it wasn't for pierced ears, he didn't know what to do with it. I demonstrated how to clip it to his stretched earlobe. He followed my instructions and, when the earring stayed affixed, he shook his head in delight to make it dangle. Then he flashed me a big, toothless smile.

When the presentations were over, we were offered rice wine—in a communal mug. This was the last thing we needed, especially since I was coming down with a nasty sore throat. But not participating would be an insult. Though one is to swig down the entire glass in a single slurp, we let Bill do the chug-a-lugging, saving one last sip at the end for me. Apparently, he wasn't concerned about contracting my cold, because he downed a few more glasses before the "music" and dancing commenced.

The Iban ladies re-entered the communal area clad in woven skirts with peasant-type blouses. Over their skirts, at the top of their midriff, they wore a type of metal coin belt with long strips of large coins, all linked together. They walked over to what appeared to be cast-iron pots. Then we realized that these were their musical instruments. Some of the women performed a slow dance to the monotonous banging and tinkling of the pots. But the entertainment picked up when the senior men of the tribe took their turns dancing. Wearing little more than a loincloth and feathered headdress, they displayed numerous tattoos all over their bodies. Moving in slow motion in crouched positions, with their arms outstretched, every now and again, they'd jump from one foot to the other, letting out a yelp that helped keep me awake.

At the conclusion of the tribal dancing, we all rose from the floor to have our photos taken with the Iban dancers. It was hard to imagine these small, somewhat emaciated people as a menace to anyone. They were so little, and friendly that we felt more of a threat, because we towered over them. Why, we could crush them if we ever fell over on someone. Then we remembered that their enemies matched them in size, and we glanced overhead at the hanging skulls.

Before long, Bill was leading everyone around the communal area in a conga line—men, women, children, all winding through the longhouse, hands on the hips of the person in front of them. They traipsed behind him to the banging and clinking on the cast-iron pots, as though they were following the Pied Piper.

Back in our "luxurious" guesthouse, we tried to get some sleep, but the evening ended up being more of a pajama party ... three of us in our "private" stalls, chatting and laughing about the evening. Sometimes, it was hard to hear each other over the noise outside—whoever thought roosters only crowed at dawn? About the time things settled down, dogs ran through the compound, barking ferociously while they chased some poor creature that let out a series of yelps—we didn't want to know what was going on outside.

Morning couldn't come soon enough for us. I opened my eyes, and saw something large and black on the outside wall of my stall. "What was it?" I wondered, not being able to decipher it without my contact lenses. I leaned closer and discovered a gigantic black spider with looooooong legs. Thank goodness he was so large, then he couldn't squeeze through the holes in the chicken coop wire that stood between the two of us, over the wooden wall.

After breakfast, Donnie asked if we wanted to go on a jungle walk. Of course we did, it was to be included in our excursion. His idea of a "jungle walk" consisted of a steep climb up the hillside to see the pepper trees. Eventually, he extended his hand to assist us in the rugged climb. On the way down, Bill asked if he was married. When hearing Donnie was single, Bill devilishly suggested that he should look for a rich wife. To make matters worse, he started telling Donnie how Shirley owned two houses. All of a sudden, Donnie became *very* attentive to both of us, grabbing us by the arms to aid us in climbing down the hillside. Meanwhile, we were ready to give Bill a push over the edge!

One last event before boarding our longboat for the return to Kuching—a blowpipe demonstration! A skinny, bent over old man with lots of tattoos put the dart into his blowpipe, and hit his target. Bill tried next, and got close. I was last, and missed my mark by a long shot—Bill was lucky this time.

Donnie was a lot friendlier on our six-hour transport to Kuching—he didn't seem to mind conversation this time. Could it be because he thought he had a fifty-fifty chance of finding himself a rich wife? We dragged ourselves into the air-conditioned lobby of the Kuching Hilton. Bill turned to me, "Remember when Donnie asked if we wanted one or two nights at the longhouse, and you said one?"

"Yes?" I answered hesitantly.

"Best decision you ever made!"

LUCY (RICARDO) AND ETHEL (MERTS) HIT HONG KONG!
HONG KONG

It was like being in an old episode of "I Love Lucy." We could make anything an issue, without any effort at all.

I think we all have a tendency to be like robots sometimes—we just go through the motions, without giving them much thought. Shirley and I exemplified it this particular morning. Our room at the Hong Kong Hyatt was directly across from the elevator bank, where there were three elevators on each side. After breakfast, we went back to the room to retrieve our cameras from the room safe.

The maid's cart was outside the door, and she was making up the beds when we entered. I smiled at her, and indicated that this was our room. Then I went over to the safe. I don't know that she understood what I was saying, but she didn't seem too concerned, because she left to clean the bathroom. Bending down, I entered the code to open the safe. Nothing happened. I repeated my efforts. Nothing happened.

"Shirley, I can't get into the safe! I tried twice. What should we do?" Getting the maid's attention, Shirley pointed to me, and I indicated that the door wouldn't open.

"Can you call security?" Shirley asked.

"Yes, yes, I call," the maid responded, picking up the phone, and muttering in Chinese.

Then, I looked at the chair to my right. What was that hanging over its back? It looked like a man's white dress shirt. I felt violated to think that there had been a man in our room—the nerve of someone making himself at home in our room, when we hadn't checked out yet! Then it was suddenly apparent.

"Shirley, we're in the wrong room!"

"What?"

"See that shirt—it isn't *mine*, and it isn't *yours*!" "Oh my god!" we exclaimed in unison.

Picking up our purses, we dashed out of the room. I'm sure the maid wondered where we'd gone, when she came out of the bathroom. Sure enough, as we dashed to the elevators, we realized that for the first time since we arrived at the hotel, we had taken the elevators on the opposite bank, and gotten our direction confused. We made certain that we were nowhere to be found when security arrived.

JOURNEY TO THE NETHERWORLD (OOPS, I MEAN ANOTHER WORLD) ...
MYANMAR 1993

As has so often been the case, several months after booking my trip, the door of the plane opens, and I step outside, after more than twenty hours of traveling. I glance around, and try to remember why it was that I wanted to come to this country in the first place. Then I reminded myself—it was somewhere new—it promised to be an adventure.

"I just received the latest State Department warning, and it says to avoid travel by plane, train, car, and bus." These were the latest words of caution from my travel agent.

"That doesn't leave us a lot of options, does it?" I tried to get her to lighten up, but to no avail.

"I'm serious, this is a dangerous place. There's fighting in the mountains."

"We're not going to the mountains."

"I just want you to know what you might be in for."

"I do, and I appreciate your concern, but would you please book us for Burma, Myanmar, or whatever they're calling the place today."

I was the first of our little party of three to arrive at Immigration. Somehow, Bill and Shirley ended up on another bus transporting them from the plane. Meanwhile, I was caught in a sea of people—all of them short, and all of them Asian. Need I say that I stood out in the crowd? There was little semblance of order. No that's too polite, it was mass mayhem, with the "little people" pushing their way towards the front of the line. As I approached the official, I began to understand why it was taking so long to process all the visitors—none of them completed their immigration forms, so the official had to fill them out for everyone.

The sense of being forsaken began to creep over me, and I was becoming nervous. After all, Myanmar is a military state, and one not particularly gracious about inviting visitors. Only the day before, I stopped at the consulate in Bangkok to see if restrictions on bringing camcorders into the country were still in effect. As usual, no one knew the answer, but everyone was eager to hold mine until my return to Bangkok. I decided to take my chances, because I was certain that if I left my most prized possession, I wouldn't see it again.

Staring ahead, I wondered if our guide was waiting for us in the other hall. Then I noticed a tiny man in a white jacket and type of sarong waving furiously. When I finally made eye contact through his round spectacles, I realized that he was motioning for me to come to the head of the line.

Looking at a ragged piece of paper that appeared to have been used, used again, and reused without benefit of the recycling process, he glanced up at me, "Your name?" When I gave him my name, he looked at the paper and asked, "You are traveling with two others?"

"Yes, another woman with red hair, and a man."

"Okay, okay, you sit over there," he said, pointing to some chairs in the waiting hall. "I find them, and help them through Immigration."

Talk about personal service. It was a pleasure to sit down and watch the local folks. The strange sounds in the crowded waiting room reminded me of chirping birds. Then I looked overhead, and high in the rafters there were lots of chirping birds. Check-in counters were opposite me, and I noticed an enormous scale by each, and they looked like they were meant for heavy freight—like cargo. I focused on people's "luggage." Anything that could hold something was enlisted for the trip. There were bags—huge plastic bags—tied at the top; there were boxes wrapped in brown paper and tied with rope; there were worn out, mismatched suitcases in loud prints and colors.

Finally, we were all together once again. Looking up at me from behind his sparkling spectacles, our guide introduced himself. "Welcome to Myanmar, my name is Fone, as in telly phone, and I'll be your guide during your stay in Yangon. You will have other guides in Pagan and Mandalay. Now, we go to your hotel."

The grounds of the hotel were lovely, on the banks of Lake Inya, but the hotel was rundown. However, as Myanmar wasn't a popular tourist destination, we really didn't expect a lot. The red carpet in our room had cigarette burns and ripples, the television worked periodically, the brown bedspreads were badly soiled, and the faded green drapes failed to close. Though the room didn't look any better in the morning, at least we were rested and anxious to begin our journey.

Fone greeted us, and showed us to our bus, a huge, old bus—just for the three of us, not counting Fone and the driver, of course. We had ample room to spread ourselves out on the tired, worn seats, so we could hear Fone's narration about his country.

Close Calls & Other Experiences 43

Not far out of Yangon, he asked if anyone wanted to change money. Guidebooks informed us about the President's fondness for the number nine; so much so, that the monetary system is based on nine. They also cautioned against exchanging too much money, and suggested beginning with twenty dollars for meals. Before we realized what was happening, Fone loosened his sarong and revealed a plastic bag tied on a string that he wore around his waist. We just stared with our mouths open, as he sat across from us so that the driver couldn't see what was transpiring. Hesitating, he reached into the plastic bag to retrieve—a *tour* brochure? We three glanced at each other, puzzled expressions affixed to our faces.

Carefully, he unfolded the worn brochure to reveal stacks of money. Clearly, his exchange rate for dollars was more favorable than the bank's, because it seemed that every time we opened our wallets over the next few days, the money multiplied.

Judging from the local populace's curiosity, we had a sense of how the first American tourists visiting China must have felt. The brown-skinned, black-eyed children were especially taken with our fair skin and red hair. "Pretty, very pretty," they said with smiling faces. Everywhere we went, people stared at us and smiled. Children offered a brown balm to put on our faces to protect us against sunburn, but we decided to rely on the good old Coppertone that we brought from home. The little children looked adorable with the lighter-colored balm rubbed on their dark cheeks and foreheads.

After several hours of driving, we arrived in the ancient city of Pagan. Approximately five thousand Buddhist temples are scattered on the banks of the Irrawaddy River, but only twenty-five hundred have been excavated. Our local guide was a young man, who led us on our tour late in the afternoon, when the temperature was more comfortable, about one hundred degrees, with ninety-eight percent humidity. We began by walking through the little town to a Buddhist monastery. It was exciting to experience an intimate, behind-the-scenes look at the life of the monks. On our stroll through town, we passed houses on stilts, with animals residing on the ground level. Local people were still at work weaving baskets, painting lacquer bowls, making furniture; and some children were stripping bamboo. They seemed delighted to have strangers from the outside world interested in their work. It also broke up the monotony of daily life in a quiet village.

Ascending the stone steps of the monastery, we left our shoes at the door, and stepped onto ... linoleum? Sometimes the linoleum was covered with newspaper—to protect it, I would assume. Glancing around the spacious but dark room, I hardly noticed the withered monk crouching on an overstuffed chair in the corner. Photos of honored or deceased monks were nailed on wooden pillars and walls. A cabinet in the corner contained cups with Queen Elizabeth II's photo on them. A page torn from a magazine depicted a train, and was taped to the wall. Curious about the "decorating," I asked our guide if there was any special significance. "Oh, no, this monk just likes anything foreign, like the cups. He also likes trains." Something furry scampered across my feet, startling me. It was a relief to learn that it was only two tiny kittens playing tag.

As the sun floated to the horizon, it was time to start our visit to the temples, when it would be cooler to climb them—perhaps ninety-seven degrees now. Each temple was more magnificent than the other, and provided wonderful photo opportunities, as they peeked at us through the trees. The valley was dotted with russet-colored stone temples that gave the illusion of being on fire in the late afternoon sun. Others were adorned with mirrors that twinkled against the deep blue skies. No wonder we nicknamed the country "Pagodaland." It looked like Asia's answer to Disneyland. Whatever imagination the Burmese lacked in decorating, they more than made up for in the various temple designs.

A panoramic view of the valley meant climbing more than one hundred steps inside the temples. Panting and perspiring, I pulled myself from one step to another. When I exited to the walkway outside, I couldn't catch my breath. This time, however, it was because of the sheer beauty surrounding me in all directions. Looking towards the Irrawaddy River, I was reminded of Luxor, Egypt. The river lazily drifted between the banks, with temples on one side, and high bluish-colored hills on the other.

The insides of the temples were different as well. One had an enormous illuminated Buddha that looked down on us. If we viewed it from one angle, it appeared to be smiling; from another angle, it was frowning. Some temples had hundreds of niches with their tiny Buddhas intact, while others were empty, because the ancient statues had been stolen for sale on the black market.

Early the following morning, we began our long drive to Mandalay, stopping occasionally for a walk through village markets. Two-seater, horse-drawn carriages were the usual mode of travel for local people—outside of walking, of course. All the wares in the markets were neatly organized and brightly colored fabrics dominated the lot. Along the dusty streets was the local version of fast food. Noodles are a prime staple among the populace, and the proprietor would grab a handful of noodles, plop them into a little bowl, and pour hot water over them. Slurp, slurp, slurp. The customers sat at a tiny Formica-topped table gulping down the hot soup. Afterwards, the dirty dishes were passed to a little girl who gave them a fast swish through some soapy water, and rinsed them off.

The drive on the "road to Mandalay" taunted us with promise of the exotic. Occasionally, our attention would be drawn to a lone temple sitting in an open field. Some of the stupas were covered with mirrors, which captured the brilliant sunlight like diamonds. Others were encrusted with actual jewels. Poor as they were, the people were generous when it came to maintaining their temples.

By the time we arrived in Mandalay, only Bill had the energy to climb the many steps to the most important temple in the city. Shirley and I were too exhausted to move one foot in front of the other. It had been a long day, and a very rough trip, particularly in the heat and humidity.

As seemed to be the custom when checking into the hotels, we were given a small piece of cardboard or a slip of paper to sign our names on. We hesitated before climbing the stone stairs, and searching for our rooms. The doors all resembled something ordinarily found on a shed, complete with a padlock. Bill's room adjoined ours, and the sounds that emanated from it when he entered reflected our own shock. He flung the adjoining door to our rooms open, and was doubled over in laughter. Noticing an open door across from my bed, I walked over and turned on the light switch.

"Hey, we have a dressing table; this is a classy place after all. And here's the air-conditioner. How do they expect the bedroom to cool, when the air-conditioner is tucked away in a closet?"

Shirley turned on the bathroom light and groaned. Bill and I rushed over for a look. The large shower didn't have a curtain, and the light only called attention to the rusty water stains that covered the shower's wall and floor.

"Mine doesn't look quite as bad, so you're certainly welcome to use it," Bill said. The only problem was that his shower didn't have a curtain either, so we had to dry off everything in the bathroom when we were finished. So, this was the "exotic" Mandalay we spent an entire day on the road to see.

The following morning, we returned to Yangon—another wonderful opportunity to fly Myanmar Air. Squeezed into our bulkhead seats, Shirley and I spent the entire flight watching a cockroach climb up the galley wall. While awaiting our departure, I overheard a tourist in the terminal announce that he was so happy the airlines had recently acquired new planes. I didn't want to think about the old ones.

Fone was waiting for us in Yangon, where the temperatures had dropped considerably from our first visit, and were almost cold compared to those of Pagan. To make matters worse, it was drizzling, and we were to visit the fabulous golden Schwedegon pagodas. The first order of business on the sacred grounds of any temple is to remove your shoes. Slipping and sliding over the marble walkways, we splashed our way through puddles, prepping ourselves for the sore throats that were certain to follow. Local people were oblivious to the weather, as they paid homage to the various Buddhas in the complex. They lighted candles and left food, cigarettes, or mementos of loved ones for the Buddha as an offering for the deceased.

As we walked the broken pavement in Yangon, we noticed dark red splotches sprinkled on the cement, like polka dots. We passed a withered old woman who spit something out of her mouth, before giving us a nearly toothless smile. At a closer look, we realized that her teeth were stained a deep red, like the splotches on the pavement. She had been chewing the infamous "beetle nut," which stained her teeth, and left the splotches behind, when discarded. From the look of the pavement, spitting beetle nut appeared to be the national pastime.

Afterwards, Fone took us to see a famous reclining Buddha. Entering the open-sided building, I lifted my camcorder to begin filming Buddha's shiny white face. The black paint all around his eyes resembled Cleopatra's eyeliner. His red lips were pursed in a smug smile, and a huge ruby was implanted between his eyebrows. I was looking at his long eyelashes, and just started recording, when a pigeon suddenly flew up one of Buddha's nostrils. It was so irreverent

Clearly, Fone was running out of things to show us, as we waited for our departure to the airport, and our return to Bangkok. Then he seemed inspired, and looked up at the three of us.

"The national dance competition is taking place at auditorium. You like to see?" Without any other options, we were at his mercy. There were many government officials in the first row of the audience, but the newspaper photographers eyed three Western tourists seating themselves during the intermission, and they rushed to photograph us instead. Relief from the popping flashbulbs finally arrived, when the performances resumed.

During the next intermission, we stood up to stretch our legs. Always mindful of our comfort, I guess Fone thought this an appropriate time for a restroom break. Seriously, he looked up at me and asked, "You go pee pee now?" His straight-forwardness caught me by surprise, but I nodded when I recovered from the shock. "Come," he said, leading me down the aisle and through the auditorium to the ladies' room.

I hadn't expected to find western facilities, with regular toilets, so I didn't have to squat into a porcelain hole in the ground. But the people were so short, that I wasn't far from the floor anyway. When I stood up, I towered over the walls of the stall. I was surprised yet again to see some local women dressed like they just returned from a shopping spree in New York. They were chattering away at the sinks, but I could sense their stares, as I walked across the restroom to wash my hands, feeling like an Amazon woman.

A few hours later, we found ourselves back at the deluxe Dusit Thani Hotel in Bangkok. We looked like rag-a-muffins in our soiled t-shirts and shorts, as we stood at the reception desk.

"I'm so sorry, but we don't have two rooms," the clerk said. "Would you mind terribly if we asked you to share a two-bedroom suite?"

If you've traveled enough, it has happened to you ...
Around the World 1997

A four-hour layover seems like an eternity, when you're anxious to get on your international flight. But one mishap, and you're praying for more time.

Who, in this day of extended travel (due to security alone), would want to take a tour around the world? Let's just say that after having spent twenty-one days flying more than twenty-four thousand miles; with thirty-six hours of airtime alone (and much more in reality), I couldn't sit down for a week! The best part was that Shirley and I had already been to London, Bangkok, New Delhi, Jaipur, Agra, and Hong Kong several times; however, Seoul was a new destination, although it was only an overnight stay. Still, at a little more than three thousand dollars, this was a bargain, and little did we know, it would turn out to be an experience in itself.

We sat in our seats on the United flight, enthusiastically planning our free time in London. Then the captain addressed us over the loud speaker, "We've just received word that there's some bad weather in New York, folks, so we're being asked to wait for take-off until we're advised from JFK." Whew, thank goodness we had four hours between our landing time and the overseas flight on Virgin Atlantic. After waiting two hours on the ground in Chicago, JFK finally cleared us for take-off. Anxiety was building, but we still had adequate time on our side.

An hour was lost, between circling JFK for a half-hour and waiting another half-hour for our bags to arrive—and then there was the half-hour trek to the international terminal. Things were now looking pretty grim, but we didn't give up hope—until we arrived at the Virgin Atlantic check-in counter, and found at least a hundred people ahead of us in line! Only thirty minutes left before the plane was scheduled to take off! Then the announcements began. The tiny ticket agent behind the counter had a big voice for her size, as she shouted repeatedly,

"There are no more seats available for this flight! Everyone will have to come back tomorrow and wait for stand-by seats."

Well, you can imagine the response she received. Passengers started protesting, as they searched their carry-on luggage for something to throw at her.

"But we have our tickets, and the flight hasn't taken off yet!"

"Yes," she quipped smugly, "but you're required to check in NO LESS than two hours before take-off, so your seats were sold." She took our names and added them to the long list for the next day's flight, and dismissed us without any compassion.

The next day, we were the first in line, arriving at 1:30 PM, although the ticket counter didn't open until 3:30 PM. As we climbed aboard the flight at 6:30 that evening, we wondered what else could go wrong ...

For starters, London was cold and rainy, as it was early November, so I climbed into a second pair of pants, and another jacket. I was as big as the Pillsbury doughboy, but at least I was warm—well, almost. Having lost a whole day, we squeezed as much into our overnight stay as possible. We bought a tour bus ticket that allowed us on/off privileges at all the historic sites. Piccadilly, the Tower of London, Knightsbridge, Westminster Abby, Harrod's, and even Sotheby's—we saw them all.

Another day of flying, before we found ourselves amidst Bangkok's golden temples, whose mirrored edifices glistened in the brilliant sunlight.

New Delhi bustled with activity and mayhem. Our young guide took our imaginations to their limits, as he portrayed the lifestyle in New Delhi during the time of the Mogul Empire. This was my third visit to India, but I never enjoyed it more, because I was seeing it in a new light. Jaipur, as always, was wonderful, and we once again rode to the Amber Fort on elephant-back; and were peddled through the streets in two-seater tri-shaws.

I felt somewhat guilty when I thought of all the people who had never seen the Taj Mahal, even the people living in India, and here I was, visiting it for the third time. But never had I seen it so magnificently. Our guide had us departing from the hotel before sunrise. I mumbled and grumbled that it was still so hazy out due to the dampness, that we'd be lucky if we could see our hands in front of our faces. Instead, I watched the Taj as if it was emerging from sleep, engulfed in the misty sunrise.

Returning to Katmandu was as exciting as ever, when our plane descended into the expansive Katmandu Valley, nestled between the Himalayas. The ancient red brick buildings with wooden ornamentation were still unique. Filming the white stupas outlined in colorful flags was a photographer's delight. Nepal still remained a remote destination, and always a place unto its own. I can't recall anywhere I've ever been that has resembled the architecture and natural beauty that Nepal has to offer. The warm sunshine and clear blue skies were a far cry from our weather in London.

Still marveling from India and Nepal's delights and the treasures, we sat on our plane to Hong Kong. The tarmac was covered with luggage, and the baggage handlers were standing around talking. Hmmm ... there was something desperately wrong with this picture. Then the plane's engines started, and we were on our way to Hong Kong—with our luggage still on the tarmac in Katmandu! Not having our clothes wasn't the worst part of the situation—having to give up an afternoon to return to the airport to claim our luggage was much worse, indeed. Since China had just regained Hong Kong, the government was insistent that everyone had to identify his or her own luggage, "in case someone wants to inspect it." So, instead of the tour operator sending a representative out to claim the luggage, all sixteen in our group had to trek to the Kai Tak Airport, sacrificing our precious free time.

We were dragged through every one of Kai Tak's terminals—up stairs, down elevators, top to bottom from one end of the airport to the other—through *all* the terminals. Our luggage was finally located, and no one was asked to identify a single piece—or open it for inspection. So much for the way the Chinese government was now running Hong Kong!

Earlier in the year, Asia's economy had fallen—a lot. Because of the change in government, everything was now outrageously expensive, with prices three to five times higher than four years earlier, when we were last there. Steak restaurants we dined in were now cost prohibitive, and we found ourselves watching our few remaining pennies. We had a quick tour of the former palace and a few shrines in Seoul, and were soon on our way back to the States.

Did I have any misgivings about taking a whirlwind tour around the world? Not in the least (well, let's qualify that answer by saying that I didn't regret it—once I could sit upright in a chair without the use of a fluffy pillow).

Five little words ...
"Remove your shoes—legs overboard!"
Baku National Park, Borneo

Who thought the boat ride would be the wildest part of our "wildlife" excursion.

Those five little words said it all. Nothing was going as expected. The tide in the river was so low that the boats might scrape the bottom, so we spent a couple of hours wandering around a Chinese temple, and through the colorful Malaysian village. The onslaught of tourists was perhaps the most exciting thing to pass through it in a long time. Finally, the water was high enough to head for the park.

Before embarking on our motorboat ride, we were each handed a life vest. Good idea, except they were meant for little Asians, not large Americans. I felt like an Amazon woman harnessed into an iron maiden. And try as I might, it still didn't zip up. At last, we were jetting down the river in great haste. An occasional wake from one of the other boats splashed us as we rolled from side to side, and bounced up and down. Like screaming little children on a roller coaster ride, Bill and I were overcome with excitement, as the ride became faster and rougher. We approached the beach where we were to land, and one last splash of water surprised us. We hustled to rescue our camera bags from a pool of water surrounding our feet.

No, it wasn't a good sign, when the boat's captain shouted for us to take our shoes off. What? Take our shoes off? Yep, he didn't intend to bring the boat any closer to shore, and we had to slide over its side into water that was nearly knee-deep. Bill rolled his pants up, but as they were already pretty wet, it wasn't much of an improvement. Still overcome with laughter, we waded ashore, proclaiming that this is what adventure travel was all about.

We arrived at the lodge just in time for a mediocre lunch. With stomachs half full, we began our jungle trek to see, as the brochure would say, "Wildlife that was indicative of the Malaysian jungles, including wild pigs, an assortment of exotic birds, monkeys—and snakes." Initially, we were enthusiastic, as we spotted three monkeys scurrying about in the bush. For a time, we walked on a wooden platform. Eventually that ended, and we found ourselves on a path through the dense tropical forest. The temperature hovered around one hundred degrees, and the humidity crept to ninety-six percent. Pushing on through the foliage, we found the path edging upward over rocks at first, then boulders, sometimes becoming a little steep. "Left, right, left, right, left …" I reminded myself to just keep putting one foot in front of the other, one foot in front of the other, one foot … what happened? Everyone stopped. What did they see? Our guide tilted his head backwards, looking up the tall trees that formed almost a ceiling over the jungle. Likewise, everyone in the group tilted their heads backwards, looking up the tall trees. Nothing. No pigs, no birds, no monkeys. All we could hear was the loud humming of bugs, until it was almost deafening. That at least told us someone inhabited the jungle—but we couldn't even see the bugs.

Reluctantly, we turned and retreated out of the jungle, along the steep path, out of breath by this time. "What do you want to bet that when we get back to where we started, all the monkeys will be lined up," I mumbled in disappointment. "They'll probably all have cameras to take our pictures, and sell them to us later this afternoon!" Well, I was partly right, because there was an assortment of monkeys right where our path began, but they were more interested in searching for crabs and bugs than taking our pictures. Our guide pointed to a green snake heavily camouflaged by the leaf it was lying on. It was one of Malaysia's most deadly snakes … I did take a photo of that small piece of Malaysian "wildlife."

When the rest of the group opted for a trek down a different jungle path, I thought it more sensible to have a seat on the bench near the water. By this time, the sun had come out, and the islands were beautiful. I sat down in the shade, where an occasional breeze would cool me off. Awhile later, the group resurfaced—they saw some lizards. I tried to make them jealous of the breeze and the view that I found. So much for the jungle wildlife—but that boat ride was worth the price of the excursion.

Hey, Ponce, Go South—and Inland!
Machu Picchu, Peru, 2005

Webster's dictionary doesn't have much to say about Ponce de Leon, except that he was a Spanish explorer who discovered Florida in 1513. If there are two things I remembered learning in high school, one was that toilets flush in the opposite direction south of the equator. The second was that Ponce discovered Florida while looking for the "Fountain of Youth." Poor guy, he was really wrong about that one—he should see the populace of the "Senior Citizen State" today, and he'd know how far off the chart he was on his exploration. I could tell him where to find the "Fountain of Youth," because I recently discovered it.

Of course, Ponce de Leon would have to sail farther south than Florida—and sail from the Atlantic to Pacific Ocean—*and* travel inland—to Peru. Yes, the Fountain is in Peru—Machu Picchu, Peru, to be precise. When I first visited Machu Picchu about thirty years ago, I wasn't concerned with the Fountain of Youth—I was young—I was always going to be young. Uh huh. In the decades since I was there, my joints turned into a Latin orchestra. When I walk up stairs, or even walk too long, my knees click like a Flamenco dancer's castanets.

The thought of climbing all those Inca ruins three decades later nearly sent me into cardiac arrest. But then again, I find myself tackling challenges on vacation that I wouldn't fathom at home. I was excited about the opportunity to visit Machu Picchu once more, placating my anxiety with the thought that I didn't have to visit *all* the ruins.

Apparently, the Inca gods were on my side, because a beautiful train operated by the owners of The Orient Express had replaced the run-down locomotive that formerly transported us from Cuzco. Comfortable seats, dome windows that stretched overhead (so we could see the tops of the Andes mountain), and a toilet that flushed (instead of depositing its contents directly on the train tracks) were a welcome relief.

Upon our arrival at the foot of Machu Picchu, we proceeded directly from the train station to the top of the mountain in small buses. Zigzag, zigzag, the former dusty road up the mountain was now well paved. We left the threat of rain behind in Cuzco, and the sun beamed overhead. Expansive, majestic, mind-boggling. The Inca ruins were all of that and more. Before I knew it, I was climbing step after step (or shall I say rock after rock, because the steps weren't always that precise) from one building to another. Up and down, up and down, stopping occasionally to catch my breath and take more photos and videos. How many times I thanked God for allowing me the privilege of a return visit. Sometimes, the trail—or stairs—took us right to the edge of the mountain. A misstep could send you tumbling over the edge. I froze at one such point, and asked a man in our group to take my hand for steadiness, until I could descend the first step. Focusing on my feet, I finally placed my foot out and stepped down. Right foot, right foot, right foot (best to use only one foot to slow myself down). I kept reminding myself not to look ahead or around me—just look at where I was putting my foot.

For three hours, I followed our guide in the mid-afternoon's heat with cameras hanging over my shoulders and around my neck, and holding my umbrella overhead for protection from the sun. Perhaps even greater than my sense of joy for having revisited one of the highlights of my years of traveling, was the joy of waking up in the morning, and feeling like a teenager. Hips didn't hurt, legs didn't cramp, and knees didn't crunch. I never felt better. To confirm that I wasn't having delusions, one of my travel companions said he was almost ready to cancel his trip, because of imminent knee surgery. But he, too, never felt better.

I couldn't have been imagining that I felt this good, could I? A week after returning home, I was in a store with my sister. We were engrossed in a conversation when, out of the clear blue, a man called out, "Miss ... Miss." No one assumed I was a "miss" in thirty years, so I didn't think he meant *me*. He persisted, and was so close that I guess I realized perhaps he was talking to me after all. "Excuse me, Miss ..." he began again. This time, he had my attention—I was waiting for him to tell me I'd dropped something, or forgotten something in my cart. Looking directly into my eyes, he said in a soft voice, "I just wanted to tell you that I think you're very pretty." I almost had to pick myself up off the floor, but it was then that I started thinking about that Fountain of Youth. The aches and pains are starting to creep back into my body parts now, but I can't deny that something very special did happen to me on that trip to Machu Picchu. A heartfelt thanks to those Inca gods!

THE ANIMALS WEREN'T THE ONLY ONES THAT EVOLVED!
GALAPAGOS ISLANDS, ECUADOR

I may have stumbled onto the ship, and tripped down the stairs, but over the next few days, a new me evolved. Grab the sunglasses, sunscreen, and sunhat. Squeeze into an all-too-small life-vest, and get ready to attack the rocky islands. Oh yes, and leave the high-heeled shoes onboard.

Of course I knew it would be hot—after all, we were sailing near the equator. By the time we boarded our ship, however, all we were looking forward to encountering was our air-conditioned stateroom. There was little time to freshen up, before we were divided into four small groups (*dolphins, frigates, boobies,* and *iguanas*), snapped into our life-jackets, and squeezed into life-boats (zodiacs) for transport to the first of several islands we'd be visiting over the next few days.

Once or twice, we had wet landings, where we slipped our legs overboard, and waded to shore. Another time, we climbed several steps from our landing to the top of the island. "Island" was a kind word for the rocks that composed the Galapagos chain. For the most part, the foliage was sparse, and the terrain very rocky, as a result of the volcanic activity. An umbrella was a welcome respite from the scorching sun, but I felt I resembled a tightrope walker, as I held it high over my head while scaling all the rocks in the pathway around the islands.

Couple balancing the umbrella with operating two—no, three cameras (a 35mm, a camcorder, *and* a panoramic), and I was shocked that the wildlife still managed to ignore me. Sea lions continued to sleep in our pathway, with an occasional youngster navigating between our feet, as we stumbled along. Land and marine iguanas took their lives in their little feet, as we inched closer and closer to them. Orange Sally Lightfoot Crabs amused themselves by climbing over the black lava rocks and diving into the ocean, while we photographed all the animals and birds, none of which acted as though they were threatened by our presence.

The most amazing feat, however, was the fact that I didn't break a leg, or even twist an ankle, as I climbed over rocks and boulders as though I was a part of the indigenous wildlife on the islands. So, Darwin performed his work on the theory of evolution in these islands, but little could he have known that I evolved from clumsy to graceful in the matter of only a few days!

CHAIRMAN MAO STILL HAS INFLUENCE ...
YANGTZE RIVER, CHINA

I've thought about my trip a lot. China had taken a 360-degree turnaround from my first visit nineteen years ago. It was clean, and modern, more modern even than our biggest cities in the U.S. But one thing was clear—even though China had moved into the new Millennium, Chairman Mao's influence was still present.

You know how you weigh the pros and cons of something, then go ahead and do whatever you want anyway? Uh huh ... I must have passed the door to the beauty shop on our ship three or four times. I kept looking at the list of services—six dollars for a haircut? My god, what did I have to lose for six dollars? I might as well splurge, and go for the wash and blow-dry as well. Things were quiet on the ship. We hadn't cruised into any impressive scenery yet, so I wouldn't be missing much, if I took a little time out for some pampering. When I make my mind up, it's full speed ahead, and I was disappointed to find another woman in the beauty shop's chair, having her hair trimmed. I saw the woman's shiny, thick, black head of hair from the back, and wondered if she was Asian, since most of the tourists were Caucasian. What would the beautician think when she saw my hair—or rather, my hair *under* my *wig*?

At last, it was time for my appointment, and I was anxious to see what the outcome would be. "Wish me good luck," I called to Shirley, as I closed the door to our stateroom, and dashed up the stairs to the beauty shop. I took my place in the chair, and asked if there was a book with photos of hairstyles.

"No."

"Oh, well, then I guess I'd like my hair trimmed to jaw length," I said, demonstrating the length. "You know how to do a 'bob'? Shorter underneath, and longer on top?" The beautician smiled sweetly. "Maybe you could 'texturize' my hair for more volume—you know, 'texturize'?" She smiled. Then I removed my wig, and released my hair, which dropped to my shoulders.

She spread my hair out, and reached for a bottle on the shelf. Squirt. Squirt, squirt, squirt. She began squirting the shampoo on my hair—my *dry* hair!!! Then she began massaging it through my hair. Did she realize she hadn't wet my hair? Rub, rub, rub, massage, massage, massage. I was more concerned with the fact that she hadn't wet my hair, than I was in enjoying the massage. It seems that the Chinese are really into massages. I had two foot massages that ended at my neck! This chick might end at my feet! At about the time when I was becoming annoyed, because I wanted to get on with the haircut, she began removing some of the lather from my head, and shaking it from her hands into the sink. "At last ... she's going to rinse me off," I thought. Then she reached for the bottle of shampoo *again*—squirt, squirt. I didn't have that much hair in the first place—and it certainly wasn't dirty enough to warrant a half-gallon of shampoo. The way she moved the lather around my head, she looked like she was icing a cake, swirling, fluffing, and puffing it.

Finally, she took me by the arm, and led me to the sink. I put my head back, and she rinsed, and rinsed, and rinsed, until all the lather washed down the drain. Then she directed me back to the chair, and began pinning my hair up off my neck. I thought it somewhat peculiar when she reached for a straight-edged razor, and started shaving my neckline, but she was the beautician—she *must* know what she's doing. After trimming my neck, she released my hair, and extended the hair on top my head. Carefully, she cut off a good three inches—wop! Well, I could afford to lose three inches, I told myself. Then she began working at the back of my head. I didn't see what she was doing, but I could sense from her actions that she was "texturizing" my hair, cutting into twisted pieces of hair, which would give me volume (at least that's what I told myself). Now, the sides—wop, wop, wop. I told her to stop "whopping," when she was heading above my ears. "I want it long enough to put into a ponytail—you know a ponytail?" I was getting desperate about this time, and I'm afraid it was beginning to show on my face.

It was a little late in coming, but I started realizing that this was a mistake, but by that time, I was at the point of no return. I looked in the mirror and told myself that everything would look better, when she blew my hair dry. "Conditioner" she said, as she squirted some gooey stuff on my head. Then she reached for the hairdryer and brush. Lift the hair, and blow it back, lift the hair, and blow it back—on top, on the sides. Lift and blow. What *was* she doing??? Now I was beginning to panic. She turned the dryer off, and smoothed the hair down—before spraying it with lacquer.

"You like?" she asked.

"Well, it's a little *short* ... "

It didn't take a genius to see that I was disappointed, even though I was forcing a smile. She looked like I'd just shot her, as she put her fingers to her mouth with that "did I do something *wrong*?" expression.

Initially, I figured that if the hairdo was halfway attractive, I wouldn't insult her by putting my wig back on, so I brought a bag to carry it back to my stateroom. Fortunately, this little Chinese beauty was one step ahead of me—she reached for my wig, placed it on my head—and started to *style* it. By this time, I just wanted to scream, "Leave your damn fingers off my wig—I can style it myself—I don't need you to mess *this* up for me, too!" Instead, *I* just smiled. I wondered if she could feel my body tensing up—I could use that massage about now. She should have waited until she was through, because *that's* when I needed to relax.

I looked at the floor around the chair—my hair was nestled around my feet—four year's worth of it. I gave her a much too generous tip and dashed out of the salon. I couldn't wait to get downstairs to my stateroom—couldn't get there fast enough, in fact. I was fleeing at top speed. Then, nearly at the bottom of the staircase, I tumbled down the last three steps—bump, bump, bump! Thank goodness my wig didn't fall off, and the floor attendant wasn't standing at her desk. When I hit the floor in one last crash, a cute little Chinese face appeared from behind the desk. The young girl was in horror, seeing me in a big lump at the foot of the stairs. I began flailing my arms about me, shouting, "I'm okay, I'm okay," as I groped for the railing to lift myself up.

Embarrassed, but considering myself fortunate that there wasn't anyone else around to see me humbled by my literal "flight" down the stairs, I limped my way to the room.

"Well, how'd it come out?" Shirley asked when I entered.

"You won't believe it—I look like Chairman Mao—with red hair!"

"It can't be that bad ..." she tried to console me.

"Thank god I have my wigs! Even my father's hair is longer, and he's nearly ninety years old!"

That night at dinner, Zhao, our tour manager was sitting next to me. Maybe I was imagining it, but he was especially attentive, and spent a lot of time looking at me. Then he spoke.

"I saw you in the beauty shop this afternoon."

"You *saw* me? Where was I? Was I sitting in the chair, or having my hair washed? I didn't see you seeing me, and I watched the door ..."

"I think you were having your hair washed" he responded to my continuous chatter. Then why was he looking at me so funny, if he thought I'd just had my hair washed?

"I was going to get a haircut, but then I saw you" he went on. I pretty much knew—he'd seen me getting my haircut, and wondered why it was still so long.

"Zhao, I have something to tell you," I began. "I've been wearing wigs on the trip, but I thought I could use a haircut—my hair was down to my shoulders, and I figured I wouldn't miss a few inches—I could use a trim." He looked at me. "Zhao, when she finished I looked like Chairman Mao! The funny thing is, I think she gave me the same haircut I saw on another woman in the beauty shop earlier in the day." He looked at me with amusement.

"I heard they only know one haircut, so that's why I hesitated."

If only *I'd* heard ...

Apparently, Shangri-La is Still Elusive ...
Lhasa, Tibet

After three visits to Katmandu, Nepal, I still had the feeling I was far away in a magical place. But Nepal isn't as remote as one might think—just ask the thousands of foreigners who trek through its mountains each year. It's hard to find a place today that still has a sense of remoteness. But somehow, I imagined I might find it in Tibet. After all, wasn't it in Tibet where the famous Shangri-La was supposed to be hidden away?

As our plane approached its destination, the snow-capped Himalayan mountaintops peeked out from the clouds, and the sunshine on their brilliant white snow made them glorious, and a thrill to capture on film. The drive to Lhasa from the airport took about an hour, giving us ample time to view the scenery on the way. The mountains around us were well above the tree line, so they were rather barren, as was the land. Small, blue lakes dotted the lunar landscape, and clumps of trees gathered around their banks.

Downtown Lhasa was a city of wide streets, but few cars. I wondered where in the mountains around us we would find the Potala Palace—the home of the Dali Lama, were he ever able to return to Tibet. Then I noticed something strange—it was a big building—a red and white structure that appeared to be on a hill, in the center of town. Could that be it? Could that be the Potala Palace? But I assumed it would be in a remote mountain area ...

Our sightseeing the following day took us to Buddhist temples that formerly housed as many as 10,000 monks. We walked the streets and markets inside the city, where we found pilgrims and local people in prayer. They spread mats out in front of them, and proceeded from a standing position, to kneeling, and finally one of prostration, and they repeated this method of adoration before images of Buddha no less than 10,000 times over the next few days.

Meanwhile, we shopped the local markets, and the Tibetan people looked at us like we were from another world. Our fair skin and red hair were of particular interest, as the local people smiled at us, and kept their dark eyes fixed on the strangers from the West. At such moments, it felt as though our world was almost non-existent. I expected to find the country as it was portrayed in the movie, *Seven Days in Tibet*, with Brad Pitt. Instead, I found Brad Pitt and Angelina Jolie's latest movie, *Mr. and Mrs. Smith*, playing at the modern local theater. And it looked like the Avon lady also made her way around the world, in hopes of finding new customers, because on the city's main street was a store selling Avon cosmetics and beauty products. Culture shock this was, for certain—in more ways than one.

Later in the day, we were in one of the many monasteries. Monks walked amidst the tourists, and the feeling of being in a remote part of the world, partaking of a spiritual practice was just about to make itself apparent. I walked from room to room in reverence, trying to focus on the majesty of the moment. Sitting on a blanket in a window box was a young monk. Nestled in his lap on a blanket was a little kitten. The monk was holding his prayer book in front of him, as the kitty slept peacefully. But there was something amiss after all ... I looked at the monk ... I looked at the kitten ... I looked at the monk again—he was talking on a cell phone!

I left the monastery disappointed. Where was I anyway—in the exotic, mysterious East, or back home in the West?

Yakety yak—I don't think I'm goin' back!
Lhasa, Tibet

Our guide said there would be railings along the way, to aid in our climb. But then he promptly added that they might be sticky from yak butter. And there would be stairs inside the palace, but they, too, might be slippery from yak butter. Yak butter, yak butter—what's the deal with this yak butter? We would find out before the morning ended.

Eventually, the lethargic feeling from the high altitude passed, and none too soon. The day had finally arrived. Today was they day we were climbing to the Potala Palace, which is to Buddhism and the Dali Lama what the Vatican is to Catholicism and the Pope. The pills for mountain sickness had done their job, and we were becoming accustomed to the more than 11,000-foot altitude. If only there was an easier way to reach the top of the palace, besides climbing.

We started our ascent at street level, and climbed the sometimes-steep walkway encircling the palace. Occasionally, there were stairs, but for the most part, it was easier than our guide had portrayed. Stopping along the way to photograph the city around us, we arrived inside a courtyard, and waited for our turn to enter the palace. Statues of Buddha were all around us, fenced in behind chicken wire. Religious murals could barely be deciphered, because of the damage resulting from the lighted yak butter candles that were everywhere we looked.

Many farmers from around the country save their money for a year or more, and group together to rent a truck to drive them all to Lhasa for their pilgrimage. Up stairs, down stairs, walking through narrow corridors, tourists mingled with pilgrims, many of whom were in native dress. Most of them carried yak butter in containers made of plastic, or wrapped in cloth or tin foil, and some even poured melted butter from bottles. They scooped it in blobs around the burning candles. If it had been marijuana they were burning, we'd have all been in a deep stooper. Instead, we just smelled the rancid yak butter. Now and then, one of the old women on a pilgrimage would drop to the ground, and prostrate herself in front of one of Buddha's images, totally oblivious to everyone around her. Up, down, up, down, over and over again, until I was exhausted just from watching her.

The "palace" can't be compared to those in Europe, but it is of significant value to the Buddhists. Our guide was trying to give us a crash course in Buddhism, I guess, but somewhere along the line, she lost us. Amidst the red benches, banners hanging from the ceiling, and the hundreds of images of Buddha behind chicken wire, we surrendered to our weariness. Shirley sat down on a pile of old, musty carpets for a rest. Meanwhile, I found a chair for my tired bones. It looked like something from a kitchen dinette set in the fifties, with chrome legs, and a red vinyl seat and back. The seat had a horrible rip in it, and the stuffing was coming out, but it still felt good to my stiffening bones. I sat down, making myself comfortable, and hoping that a monk wouldn't shoo me away, because I was sitting in his chair. In front of me were lots of flickering candles, much like votive lights in a church. I watched their flames dance, as I kept an eye on the melting yak butter in which they were standing. I was going through the actions of touring the palace, but I had to keep reminding myself of where I was—in what was probably Tibet's most photographed treasure—the Potala Palace! Looking all around me at the worn carpets, blackened murals, hanging banners, statues of Buddha, candles, and the smell of yak butter, I couldn't help but wonder, was Richard Gere *really* ever here?

Back in my hotel room later that day, I stepped into the bathroom and closed the door to change for dinner. What was that horrible smell? I sniffed, and I sniffed, and I was about to gag, when I realized that *I* was the one who smelled! Apparently, everything from head to toe had absorbed the horrible smell of rancid yak butter.

"MISHAP" IS A TITLE DULY EARNED ...
CABO SAN LUCAS, MEXICO, 2006
Sometimes, nothing seems to go right—but at least things aren't boring.

Day 1 ... Got off to a good start, when checking in at the USA 3000 ticket counter. Dragging my leopard-print suitcase behind me, and struggling with my carry-on luggage, I slid my passport and documents over the counter—straight *off* the counter—and into the trash bin. My new passport hadn't even been used, and there it was, tucked away with the rubbish.

"Oh! I'm sooo sorry," I blurted out in astonishment. The agent just glared at me, and disappeared through a door. Minutes later, he reappeared, to complete checking Shirley in, without any mention of my passport, and how to retrieve it. Finally, a supervisor arrived on the scene, key in hand. He unlocked the door to the trash area (I didn't know the trash was important enough to be locked away), and smiled as he handed me my passport, graciously accepting my apologies.

Having been checked in, I dragged my dead leopard suitcase to the x-ray machine a few steps behind me, banging a few other passengers in the crowd along the way. "I'm sorry," became my phrase for the day.

Day 2 ... Where was the sun? I thought we left the doom and gloom back home in Chicago, but it managed to tag along. Oh well, a good excuse to go souvenir hunting, instead of lying around the pool. The short walk to San Jose resulted in two blisters that lasted for the entire week in Mexico, and managed to hang around another week at home. So much for wearing my thong sandals that were so comfortable last summer. Guess I'll have to remember that until those little appendages manage to puff up, I'd better stay with more reliable footwear.

Day 3 ... The sun came out, and we headed for the pool. The constant breezes kept the clouds away, but brought out the goose pimples. Suffice it to say that I didn't need sunscreen—I hid beneath my tiger print beach dress the entire day. The cool weather was a good excuse to do so, which saved me from horrific embarrassment, as I watched the young women on college break strut their stuff in itsy-bitsy bikinis. I don't know about the other middle-aged women around the pool, but I spent the entire time trying to figure out how they managed not to lose their balance, with all that silicone.

"Shirley, look at that one over there, the blonde in the green bikini. Those aren't real. I know, because if they were, her neck would be down to her waist. She doesn't even jiggle when she walks—believe me, if those were real, there would be *some* movement. And another thing ... those tiny straps tied in back would never support her, if they were real."

Day 4 ... Finally, some sightseeing—a city tour of San Jose and Cabo San Lucas. Things went pretty well. The sun was out; the sky was clear blue. The twenty-minute drive to Cabo along the ocean was fairly scenic. The glass-bottom boat trip to the "rocks" (Cabo's famous picturesque landscape) went pretty well. I squeezed into a life-vest made for a pre-pubescent child, and tried to retrieve my two cameras from around my neck to take some videos and photos. Then, about the time we arrived at the rocks, and I wanted to shoot the pelicans and seals (with my cameras, of course), the water became pretty rough. I tried to balance myself, as I took my pictures, and considered the ride a success—until, I bent over, and my sunhat flew onto the glass bottom—into some water.

Day 5 ... Time to relax around the pool. The weather was warmer, and the sun must have scorched my brain—or maybe it was all those frozen Margaritas. Shirley and I stopped by the ladies' room, before heading for the jewelry store at our hotel. I straddled the toilet, and felt something splashing around my ankles ...

"Oh my god!!!! Shirley, hand me some paper—quick—I forgot to lift up the seat cover!"

Day 6 ... At last, our day-trip north to La Paz, a former capital of the Baja Peninsula, which I figured would give us a good chance to observe the landscape. Cacti, hills, more cacti, more hills, dry ground—referred to, I believe, as "desert." The brochure promoted this tour as "the most spectacular tour of the south tip of Baja Peninsula: history, culture, art, and much more you will find in this amazing trip."

After driving for a few hours, we arrived in El Triunfo, a historical mining town. It was almost a ghost town. We proceeded to a factory to see how they weave blankets, but the weaver didn't weave on the day of our tour, so there wasn't any demonstration. Move onto the cathedral, part of an old mission built in 1861. By this time, I didn't feel like climbing out of the bus for still another disappointment, so I skipped the mission.

Maybe things would improve on the way back to Cabo, during our stop in Todos Santos, described in the brochure as "this incredible oasis: 'Hotel California', old mission, and shopping time." We were perhaps twenty minutes from Todos—and I was in the middle of a conversation with one of the other members of the tour—when our bus slowed down, and down, and down—until it stopped completely, along the side of the road. I kept on talking, when I realized something was going on. The driver and guide hopped off to check the motor. One tried to start the motor, as the other eyed it up. Before we knew it, they were declaring that we had a serious problem—the bus simply would not start. Nada. Nothing. Neither a burp nor a grunt. All the tour passengers climbed off, and stood in the shade of the cacti. Cars passed by ... no one stopped; buses passed by ... no one stopped; a truck passed by, and gave us his horn.

Thank goodness the guide had a cell phone, because he called the tour company's office in La Paz, and they sent someone to look at the engine. Of course, he wasn't any help, so arrangements were made for a public bus to pick us up along their way. Sure enough, a big bus pulled up alongside the road, its curtains tightly closed. I climbed the steps, and found the bus full of sleeping bodies. Shirley and I found a seat together, so she took a nap, like our Mexican neighbors, and I watched a video of the movie *The Village*. I couldn't understand a word of Spanish, but I was beginning to get the gist of the storyline, when we arrived in Todos, "an incredible oasis: 'Hotel California', old mission, and shopping." I could care less about the "Hotel California," didn't even see a mission in that part of town, and was disappointed in the shopping once again. Our eleven-hour sightseeing tour got us back to the hotel ninety minutes late, and exhausted.

Day 7 ... Our last day. Blisters were well bandaged, but still sore. I'm embarrassed to say it, but I was the only tourist in Cabo wearing long pants to hide my knee-high stockings (necessary to keep my shoes from rubbing my sore feet). What a picture I must have been—*underexposed*!

Day 8 ... Hate those charter flights. "Check the time on the bulletin board," our travel documents and Apple representative told us. Well, we checked, and the departure time remained as we were initially informed. Thank goodness for talkative women in the ladies' room, or we'd have never heard the "rumor" that our flight was going to depart two hours later, and the bus for the airport would pick us up an hour late.

We waited and waited, and the bus finally arrived. The airport was small—*very* small. As a result, the ticket agents also handled the immigration procedures, writing down all the information on our passports—by hand—on a piece of paper. And, of course, there weren't any x-ray machines for our luggage, so every piece of checked baggage had to be hand-inspected. We sat there for at least two hours, waiting for our flight to board; and the whole time, one of the college kids on spring break talked, and talked, and talked, without ever coming up for a breath. I decided to call home to let the family know about our long delay, so they wouldn't be worried if they tried to contact me. Little did I know that, since I didn't have a long-distance calling card, my phone call home (which lasted less than three minutes) came up as a fifty-dollar charge on my phone bill!

By the time we landed in Chicago (four-and-a-half hours later, and over two hours late) and I dropped Shirley off, it was 6:15 AM. I headed east, and the sun was brilliant—a huge red ball, right on the horizon. A wispy cloud floated across the middle of the ball. More clouds were in the background, giving the appearance of mountains. I looked at that magnificent sunrise, and immediately thought of Japan, the "land of the rising sun." The clouds behind it were etched in white, as though the mountains were snow-capped. And the mountain centered directly behind the ball came to a point, giving the appearance of Mt. Fujiyama. "Japan," I mused to myself, "I haven't been there in almost twenty years. Maybe it's time for an encore."

Chapter 2
Hotels, Lodges and Camps

The good, the bad, and the ugly!

Now you know how Cinderella felt—one day you're in a former palace; the next, you're ready to scrub the floors yourself! Words in the guidebooks like "charming" and "quaint" might be giving you a warning. Oddly enough, it's memories of the "bad" or "ugly" hotels that have stuck in my mind. They lend themselves to the most colorful stories. For instance, if you relate an experience in a beautiful hotel or resort, someone always has to do you one better about the five-star establishment they stayed in. But how many are willing to admit to ... well, shall we say more "modest" accommodations.

I FELT LIKE A PRINCESS—
BUT I COULD HAVE USED A BETTER "THRONE" ...
Cairo's Mena House, 1976

The dimly lit brass lanterns in the hall leading to the main dining room cast lace-like shadows on the high arched ceiling, causing the atmosphere to become even more exotic. I felt as though I was floating down the corridor in my glamorous new Egyptian caftan. Glancing around the dining room, with its carved lattice screens, I couldn't help but feel I was part of the Middle Eastern décor.

Several hours later, I returned to my room. As I drew the drapes, I paused to gaze at the shadow of the pyramids in the distance.

It soon became apparent that some things in "modern" Egypt weren't always as hearty as those of ancient origins. For instance, the plumbing left much to be desired. The toilet may have looked like it was from the 21st Century, but it was most reluctant to flush. Grabbing a tall glass on the vanity, I deposited at least a gallon of water in the flush box, before I had any cooperation from the porcelain fixture.

The next morning, I looked at the toilet again, trying to decide if using it was really a necessity, or just a habit after a full night's sleep. What to do? Should I use it? Would I even have time to wait for a flush before departing for the airport? Spotting the plastic wastebasket under the vanity, I placed it inside the bathtub and filled it half way with water. Lifting the lid off the flush box, I poured the water inside. Reaching for the toilet's handle, I pushed it down hesitantly. The toilet sounded like it was coughing, then choking. Ahhhhh, it was just flushing—at last!

A QUIET HOTEL IN AN INCONSPICUOUS BORDER TOWN—
ALL WAS NOT WHAT IT SEEMED ...
KIRYAT SHMONA, ISRAEL, 1976

A few of us decided to take a stroll around town before dinner, but we found it difficult to navigate the sidewalks. "Looks like they need to do a little resurfacing in this town," I remarked, glancing at the potholes in my path. The town itself was very quiet. Considering it was late afternoon, there weren't any people on the street—except the four of us.

The tour brochure read, "In Tiberius, you'll be staying at the picturesque Sea of Galilee, where you'll have a special seafood dinner." The Sea of Galilee was beautiful, indeed, and Tiberius was a very popular town, especially for the tourists, which seemed to be our problem.

"I just received word from our office, that we're unable to stay in Tiberius for the night," our tour director informed us, "so we'll be driving a little way from here to another town for this evening."

This town had a very strange name. In fact, I never forgot it—Kiryat Shmona. It was a border town near Lebanon, but we had no way of knowing that at the time. The name of the town wasn't all that was strange; our hotel was a little peculiar as well. I noticed the dark drapes over the windows. The side that faced the street was black. I assumed that it was to keep out the strong Mediterranean sunlight.

After dinner, we decided to go to the hotel's discotheque, located on the lower level, or what appeared to be the basement. I thought it odd that all the walls were covered with shag carpeting. But it *was* the '70's, and shag carpeting was everywhere, so this place was right in style. We concluded that the intent of running it up the walls must have been to keep the sound of the music from disturbing anyone. Only our little group was staying in the hotel, in this nearly deserted town. It was certainly off the beaten track from the other tourists (who were now eating *my* seafood dinner, and sleeping in *my* bed in Tiberius, overlooking the Sea of Galilee), and it was pretty quiet in the discotheque.

Years later, I was watching a program about Israel, and the various incursions on its cities. When I heard the narrator mention the name "Kiryat Shmona," my ears perked up. This town, only nine miles from the Lebanese border, was the site of one of Israel's bloodiest massacres by terrorists in 1974. Now the strange decorating in our hotel in that quiet little town with the broken sidewalks made sense. The curtains were for blackouts, and the discotheque had been an air raid shelter!

~ FAST FORWARD ~

TIMES PASSES, BUT SOME THINGS NEVER SEEM TO CHANGE ...
KIRYAT SHMONA, ISRAEL, 2006

It's funny how you never forget some things ... the war between Lebanon and Israel was as at its peak in the summer of 2006. Then one night on the evening news, I heard the name of that town I'd visited thirty years ago, Kiryat Shmona. Once again, the bombs were landing. I wondered how much the town had moved ahead in all these years, and then I realized that for some people in some places, things never really seem to change.

SOME THINGS ARE BETTER LEFT TO THE IMAGINATION ...
NEW WINTER PALACE, LUXOR, EGYPT, 1976

Eventually, I located my room, down a dark corridor. Entering it, I noticed the scarcity of furniture—and what was there was older than King Tut, and very worn.

Perhaps if the word "new" were omitted from the hotel's name, it wouldn't have been so misleading. Or, they could have called the annex the "Newer" Winter Palace. After the initial surprise was over, I was still delighted to be walking through the lobbies and lounges of the same hotel Howard Carter occupied during his search for King Tut's tomb in the early 1920's. I imagined him relaxing in one of the large velvet chairs in the lobby, perhaps reading a newspaper while a tall, wispy palm on the plant behind him peeked over his shoulder.

In retrospect, however, and with further reflection, since this was a really old country historically, the furniture must have been new by comparison. The same could be said for the hotel's name "New Winter Palace." But "new" compared to what, the pyramids?

Always looking for something positive, I was delighted to see that my room was air-conditioned, because daytime temperatures reached 115 degrees in the afternoon here in "Upper Egypt." I flipped the air-conditioning switch on the wall. A red light turned on—but not the air-conditioning. Guess I'd have to resort to the ceiling fan for comfort.

I had a corner room with two balconies, each of which was large enough to hold two people and a cricket, but not at the same time. Walking to the French doors, I opened them for ventilation. Before me flowed the Nile and a priceless view of the ancient temples of Karnak and Luxor in the distance. The street was nearly void of people in the hot afternoon sun, but a few horse-drawn buggies crept slowly up and down the dusty avenue, carrying tourists too anxious to begin their own explorations to allow the heat and flies to detain them. When the sun set later that afternoon, the temples glowed as if they were on fire, and the activity on the Nile began to settle down.

Before retiring, I peeked outside my door. The old Egyptian man in a djalaba and red fez still sat on his wooden chair, his purpose never known, although he watched me every time I left my room. When bedtime came, I glanced around to see what I could place in front of it for additional protection. The old dresser was too heavy, and the big, tired-looking green velvet chair in the corner was too awkward to drag around the double bed. The scratched wooden coffee table caught my eye, so I slid it over.

Dare I leave the balconies' French doors open? The air would still be stifling, even though the moonlight replaced the scorching sun. I entertained the idea that someone could climb from balcony to balcony without much difficulty, and enter my barricaded room while I slept. The decision was quite plain—I'd sleep with one eye watching the balcony. The sun did not rise soon enough!

HOTELS FOR EVERY TASTE—TUNISIA OFFERED IT ALL (AND MUCH MORE) ...
GAFSA, NEFTA, AND MATMATA, TUNISIA

I took a wrong turn, opened what I thought was the door to my cave, and walked in on four Spanish photographers.

It was September, and what was supposed to be the height of the tourist season. But what no one told us was that the tourists were almost exclusively French. Not only couldn't we speak to the local people, but we couldn't even converse with the other tourists. After a rough start leaving Tunis, when our rental car broke down, we finally found ourselves back on track. The Hotel Jugurtha in Gafsa was awaiting our arrival.

After settling in our rooms, Chris and I headed for the dining room, descending a stairway that was enclosed on all four sides, but open to the blue sky above. Suddenly, what we assumed were birds flew overhead, as though caught in a wind tunnel. Their shrill whistling and a loud buzzing sound were echoing in the stairwell, like something from Hitchcock's movie, *The Birds*. Watching them in flight, it was as though their landing gear was in desperate need of repair, as they flew aimlessly above us, with no apparent sense of direction. We weren't seated very long at our table in the dining room, when a swarm of them came flying through the open doors, and soared very low over the heads of the French tourists, exiting the room through the doors on the other side. By the time this encounter concluded, we realized that those weren't birds we'd been seeing, they were bats!

That evening, the air-conditioning in our rooms wasn't working, so we dragged our mattresses out onto our balconies. Sounded like a good idea. The cool evening breeze made sleeping on the balcony more comfortable, and when it swept through the palm trees, it sounded like waves on the seashore. I was just about to fall asleep, when the image of a bat tangled in my hair came to mind. I buried my head under the blanket for the remainder of the night.

On our drive south, we crossed the Chott el Djerid, the salt flats where the movie *Star Wars* had recently been filmed, finally arriving dusty and exhausted at the Sahara Palace Hotel in Nefta. The young man behind the registration desk promptly greeted us with cool drinks, and asked for the car keys, so he could give the car a complimentary wash. It didn't take long for us to climb into our swimsuits and retreat to the huge pool that overlooked the oasis. The quiet and stillness were eerie. Here was a beautiful hotel at the edge of an oasis, and it was as though we were the only two people on earth, because the hotel was nearly empty—where were all those French tourists we'd been encountering everywhere? As the sun was about to set, we drove down to the oasis in search of a Bedouin with whom we might cut a deal for camel rides through the palm groves. We bargained with the owners for our rides, proud of ourselves for making a good deal with the locals. Occasionally, the boys leading our camels would reach up and pick figs for us from the palm trees. Then we heard something approaching us through the palms. We stopped and listened carefully—we were alone with only the camel boys. What ... what was it we heard? The sound was suddenly familiar—it was the French tourists! Where had *they* come from? Guess our idea of a camel ride at sunset wasn't so unique after all.

The following day, we drove through more lunar-type landscapes, and found ourselves in Matmata, literally sleeping in a hole. The inhabitants of Matmata are *troglodytes,* or cave dwellers. Chris read about one little "hotel" that was used in *Star Wars,* so we set out in search of it. For six dollars a night, it included dinner, *and* we each had our own cave for the night. Apparently, this establishment was Luke Skywalker's house in the movie, and I wondered if he slept in my cave. Once again, we appeared to be the only guests.

It was still early in the afternoon when we arrived, and the sun was at its peak. I thought it best to take a nap, so I pushed open the wood door (and I'm talking real "wood," because it looked like it was still a part of the tree). There were two cots with clean linens, one tree stump with a dozen candles on top, and a dirt floor—so hardened that it was like cement. It was much cooler in my cave (which is, of course, the point of being a "cave-dweller"), so I slept well for a few hours.

When I awoke, I looked around for Chris, but I couldn't find him anywhere. I walked above ground, and took a stroll down the road. Some villagers were holding a celebration up ahead. I could see them dancing, and the women joined in with their high-pitched chanting. Disappointed at not finding him—and somewhat worried—I returned to our hotel to await his return. Our car was still parked outside, so that was a good sign. After all we'd been through on this trip, I didn't know what I would do if something happened to him—or me—if he didn't return. Suddenly, Chris came bursting into the courtyard.

"You really missed a great time! I took a walk, and found the villagers celebrating. They motioned for me to join them, so I started dancing along. Then the men began swinging their rifles over their heads, and occasionally they'd shoot them off!"

He was ecstatic at being a part of the action, this tall, husky, brown-haired, pink-skinned American. I'm sure the local people wondered where on earth *he* had come from (while he assumed that he fit right in).

After a sparse dinner (what can one expect for six dollars *and* a room—sorry, cave), I searched for the bathroom accommodations. To my surprise, there were flush toilets, sinks, and real showers. The only snag was that they were community washrooms. Up to this point, I didn't see much of a problem, because Chris and I were the only guests. However, later that night, I had to use the washroom. I'd taken my contact lenses out, and didn't have glasses, so I could only hope to find my way to and from the "facility." I squinted in the darkness, and tried to remember the layout of the grounds. The cave quarters were in a circle around an open courtyard that looked up to the black, star-filled sky—it was like being at the bottom of a bowl. The bright moonlight guided me to the corridor with the toilets. On my way back, however, I took a wrong turn, opened what I thought was the door to my cave, and walked in on four Spanish photographers. I don't know who was more surprised, but I made a hasty retreat, backtracked, and found my own cave. Once inside, I pushed a large boulder against the door.

"There," I said to myself, "that should keep any intruders out." Maybe I spent just a little too much time in the sun after all.

A PERSONAL "OUT OF AFRICA" EXPERIENCE ...
LITTLE GOVERNOR'S CAMP, MASAI MARA, KENYA, 1982

We zipped ourselves in and out, top to bottom, and all across the floor to prevent uninvited visitors, such as monkeys, spiders, snakes ...

My first inkling that I might be in trouble was when the young African man loaded my pink luggage on board the rowboat, and the water level of the muddy Mara River settled about six inches below the edge of the boat. I should have resisted that set of wooden bookends that I bargained for at a roadside stand; but then again, after all the other wooden souvenirs I purchased along the way while on safari, I don't think they made that much difference. To complicate matters, our rowboat didn't have oars. Instead, our "captain" pulled the tiny vessel with the three of us across the river using a rope tied from trees on one bank to trees on the other. A good deal of skill was involved not only in crossing, but keeping the boat from sinking.

But cross the river we did, and awaiting us on the other bank was a small group of tents. They weren't ordinary tents, they were *deluxe*. In addition to our well-mattressed cots, we had a dressing table with a small cracked mirror, a gas heater/lantern and, best of all, our own shower and toilet facilities in a tent adjacent to our sleeping tent—just another zip away.

Out front, directly below us, was a huge swamp, complete with Cape Buffalo. Fortunately, they were at the far end of the bank. We proceeded to the bar for cocktails before lunch, which was served outdoors in the shade of the trees, and with linen tablecloths.

Lunch finished, an opportunity for a few pictures of "life in the wilderness ... roughing it," and it was time to cross the river again to begin our afternoon game run in a four-wheel-drive jeep. Every game run was special in some way—perhaps it was a particular encounter with a black-maned lion; being encompassed by a herd of elephant; waiting for hippos to surface above eye level in their pool; or catching the sapphire sky bowing to the burnished earth, while the sun gently dipped to the horizon and burst into fiery gold behind the black outline of the acacias.

This game run, too, was special. Following the other vehicles, we noticed they'd gathered in a circle around some foliage. The shadows, combined with the rocks in the center, served to hide the identity of the long, sleek leopard. But he *was* there. Only feet away, dangling from the limb of a tree, was his dinner—a freshly killed impala. Glancing over his shoulder, the leopard called an end to the show, disappearing into the thicket.

It was preparing to rain again, and the temperature dropped considerably. The jeep cut through the plains of the Masai Mara with great speed, passing elephant and impala, zebra and giraffe along the way. A male lion sat on the dirt hill as though he was protecting his throne. We had seen it all on this wonderful eleven-day safari. But there was always one more thing to see. This time, it was a pack of fourteen hyenas. Young and old alike, they hunched defiantly, glaring at the jeep. Ugly as they are, with rounded ears and low hindquarters, scruffy coats with splotches of brown and black, even they are cute as young. And the young, small as they were, boldly stared at the intruders in the vehicle, hiding now and again in their den or peeking at us from behind tall grass. The foul stench of the scavengers pervaded the air, and we headed back to camp.

It was good to climb into the shower—the water had been warmed for us while we were on our run. The tent's flaps were dropped, and the rain was beating down on the sloped top, which was guarded somewhat by the tall trees of the forest. It was quite dark in the tent; the lantern provided our only light. Daniel, a tall African who worked at the camp, called for us to escort us to the dinner tent. He assured us that he would be on watch until morning for any animals that might be around our tent; and before breakfast, he would bring us our tea.

Daniel led us to the bar for cocktails, and we quickly became acquainted with Brian, a young Englishman, whom we asked to join us for dinner. It was exquisitely served, complete with sherry, candlelight and, of course, a crisply pressed white linen tablecloth. It seemed somewhat untimely and out of place, however, when the waiter sauntered up to the table at the conclusion of our dinner, and presented us with hot water bottles, as though they were gifts to be cherished. Bewildered at first, we burst into laughter after he left, eventually realizing that they were meant to keep our feet warm under the covers.

When breakfast concluded the following morning, I walked over to the "office" tent to settle my bill. As in many of the old movies I'd seen set in Africa, a rather scruffy elderly Englishman and his wife were in charge. A very large old-fashioned typewriter sat on a beat-up wooden desk, and an even older short-wave radio hummed in the background. Our hostess was upset, declaring that "Windy" had broken into the kitchen during the night (the third time in five days) to steal bread and biscuits. She was even more disturbed, because the cook didn't store the bakery in the freezer.

Inquiring about Windy's identity, I learned that she was an elephant. Then I was whisked away to the kitchen to see the mess she left behind. I could imagine myself running such an operation, encountering the same problems. These people had lived in Africa most of their lives, and they still loved it. I was envious of their experiences, unruly elephants and all.

LIVING LIKE A MAHARAJAH ...
SARISKA, INDIA, 1990

India has much to offer. This experience was but another facet on the prism.

The drive from New Delhi to the maharajah's former hunting lodge was long, so we departed early in the morning, giving us ample opportunity to see the countryside and many colorful villages, while sneaking a catnap or two on the side. At last, we arrived at the lodge. We climbed the steps of the long white stone building, and passed though the elegant arches. A mangy stuffed tiger greeted us in the foyer. Our rooms were clean and comfortable, but certainly not extravagant—no wonder the maharajah had to turn his hunting lodge into a hotel.

After settling in, Shirley, Bill, and Karen got together in my room to discuss our plans for the remainder of the afternoon. "Oh my god!" Karen shouted, as she pointed to the night table between the beds. Standing on its hind feet in total fright was a tiny, tiny (and I do mean *tiny*) mouse. Her shouting scared the daylights out of the poor little creature, and he jumped off the table. I promptly reached for the phone to tell the receptionist that we needed someone to remove a mouse from my room. In what seemed like seconds, two turbaned men arrived, armed with dishcloths. My friends and I looked at each other quizzically, as the staff meandered throughout the room, whisking their cloths off furniture—to no avail, of course. The poor frightened mouse was probably clinging to the bedsprings.

When things settled down, we strolled the grounds, where we saw many wild parakeets with long tails flying from tree to tree, their bright green color dazzling in the brilliant sunshine. We relaxed on the veranda with some soft drinks before dinner. Dinner? Now that was an interesting subject. There were no menus, but the waiter said we could have *anything*, "no problem." In India, *nothing* is a problem. Judging from the scarcity of guests, it was fair to assume that we could have *anything* within modest means. Deciding not to take any chances, everyone settled on tomato and cheese sandwiches and Cokes. Not only did we have the whole dining room to ourselves, we had the whole lodge to ourselves, because outside of a family of five Indian people, who came there for the weekend, we were the only guests.

Early the next morning, we were to have a game drive through the park—hopefully, to find the elusive tigers, the point of visiting Sariska, a tiger preserve. Instead, we encountered numerous peacocks—all without tails. How were we to know that they shed their tails every year! To make matters worse, they were female peacocks, and a dull brown. Not only weren't they attractive, but they weren't particularly photogenic either. The spotted deer were ample enough, jumping to and fro in the shaded fields. There were plenty of samber, a large antelope-like animal, and a favorite meal of the tiger. But perhaps the most fun were the monkeys. As we drove through rocky areas, shaded by plentiful trees, the monkeys screeched as they sprung through the trees, and swung from the branches overhead like Tarzan himself. Our driver listened to the sounds of the wild, and detected a samber calling out. It must be fearful of a tiger, so we headed off in the samber's direction. Sadly, we didn't get to see our tiger, but we certainly heard him in the bush. Apparently, he found the samber before we did.

Each time we returned to the lodge from a morning or afternoon game drive, the entire staff stood on the top step, waving furiously to welcome us back. By the fourth time, we started to feel like the maharaja himself, as they were attentive to our every wish. Many years later, I was watching a program on public television about the tiger hunts in India during the period of the British Raj. Tens of thousands of these beautiful animals had been massacred. The program spoke of the maharajas and how they hunted, taking hundreds of local men out with them, beating drums to scare the tigers out into the open to be shot. On the wall of one of the lodges was a photo of the hundreds of people who took part in the tiger hunt, as well as the hundreds of dead tigers. I recognized the picture—it hung outside my room at the Sariska Lodge.

Africa—A Land of Contrasts—and This is Just the Camps!
Botswana and Zimbabwe, 1992

Our guide warned us about being careful to check for hyenas in the bathroom facilities before walking inside. We thought he was kidding, until we asked him what the scratches were on the toilet seat.

I was pretty impressed with Moremi, our first destination in Botswana. Though the bathroom facilities in our camp were a short distance from our tents, across a path, rather than adjacent to the tent, they were amazingly large, and each tent had its own facilities. The walls of the bathroom were bamboo, and the floor was cement; but best of all, there was no roof, so the brilliant sunlight came streaming down. There was quite a glare in the mirror over the bamboo vanity, however, so it was necessary to keep my sunglasses on while trying to touch up my make-up, but one learns to deal with those sorts of things while in the bush. The good news was that we had a flush toilet and shower. I heard something outside our tent one night. Peering out the window flap, I saw my friend Bill in his pajamas, walking gingerly across the path in the bright moonlight to use the bathroom. Apparently, constructing it without a roof was a smart idea—at least he could find his way around.

Our next camp in Savuti didn't allow for private facilities, but we did have one for men, and one for women. As there were only three men and five women in our safari group, plus a male guide and female cook, this didn't present a problem, because we picked numbers to take our showers at night. Our guide informed us that the hyenas sometimes come into camp to drink the water out of the toilets, and that the scratches on the seats were from their teeth. It didn't make us feel any safer when he went on to say that their jaws were so strong that he had seen one carry off a large soft drink cooler. If we hadn't felt we were out in the bush at the last camp, there was no doubt now. One of the things I enjoyed most about the camp at Savuti was taking a shower while looking out a large window-like opening in the bamboo wall, and watching the wild game in the distance on the prairie.

The facilities in each of the camps became a little more rustic, as our safari progressed. By the time we came to Chobi in the Kalahari Desert, the camp hands were constructing a shower in a canvas tent. There was a mat on the floor to stand on while showering under a large canvas bag of hot water—warmed by the camp hands over the fire. Adjacent to the shower was a small dressing area with a folding chair on which to place our clothes and towel. I have no finer memories than standing beneath the showerhead, looking up into the black African sky at the numerous twinkling stars. "If my mother could see me now," I thought night after night, while enjoying the sparse facilities of the camps.

One thing we didn't enjoy in Chobi, however, was the toilet. We'd certainly come a long way from the flush toilets of Moremi and Savuti. Chobi's toilet amounted to a chair that resembled a lawn chair, with a toilet seat on it—over a "long-drop loo," as the British refer to it. Actually the chair was over a hole in the ground—and this "long-drop loo" had a very short drop, if you get my drift. This "modern wonder" was inside a canvas tent just large enough to zip up around you. The problem was that the temperatures hovered a little over a hundred degrees, making it ghastly hot—and we won't even mention the aroma. Of course, we could leave the tent unzipped, only it faced the road. Granted, traffic wasn't particularly heavy, but one had to make a choice between modesty and necessity—sometimes, I opted for a bush or rock when nature called.

By the time we'd reached Victoria Falls, and the very small Illala Lodge, we certainly had some cleaning up to do. I was glad to have a room to myself for a change, especially as I climbed into a big tub of hot water. It felt wonderful to wash my hair and scrub the dirt from beneath my nails. I was even glad to have the opportunity to set my hair in the curlers I dragged all the way from home. Up to this time, I'd been tucking my hair under a canvas hat every day, because it was useless to try to do anything with it while we were in the bush. Walking into the bedroom, I was delighted to find a hairdryer on the vanity. "Won't everyone be surprised to see me with a nicely styled hairdo for a change," I thought to myself, as I turned on the dryer. I flipped the switch for a blast of hot air. About five minutes into the process, the dryer went dead—no electricity. I turned the switch on and off—no electricity. I turned on the television—no electricity. NO ELECTRICITY? How could there be no electricity, when Victoria Falls was practically across the street! Victoria Falls is twice as wide as Niagara Falls, and one-and-a-half times as high! Didn't this country ever hear of harnessing the water for electricity? There I sat, curlers in my wet hair—what was I to do now? Apparently, this being the dry season, electricity from the falls was restricted to certain times of the day, because awhile later, the electricity was back on, and the hairdryer was in operation again.

It felt good to primp up and put on a pretty skirt and blouse for our last dinner as a group. I've stayed in some fabulous hotels around the world, but now they're only a vague memory. What I'll never forget, however, are those Botswana "bathrooms"!

~ FAST FORWARD ~

ELEVEN YEARS LATER ... I'M GLAD FOR THE LUXURY!
BOTSWANA AND ZIMBABWE, 2003

A safari has so much to offer, and the animals are only one part. Living in the bush can also be exciting. Whether you're in temporary camps that move with the season, or deluxe camps, there's something so special about living among the animals in the wilds of Africa that make the experience one you want to have over and over again. I'm just happy that being more than a decade older, the last time wasn't quite so rustic ...

I walked up the ramp leading to the wooden platform that held our "tent." The walls were canvas, with a high ceiling, and it was probably fifty feet by fifty feet—hardly fitting the word "tent." As I unzipped the screened entrance flap, a king-sized bed was directly in front of me, with a chair and standing lamp on my left, and a desk and chair to my right. White bath towels had been arranged on the bed's white coverlet in a design, intermingled with a leafed twig that held a hand-written note card welcoming us to Vundumtiki, in Botswana's Okavango Delta. This was a big change from our first visit to Botswana!

It was already very obvious that our accommodations on this safari were becoming more deluxe with every camp. Behind the bed was an ebony wall that served as a headboard, with a shelf in front that held lamps on each end. Over the four screened panels of the canvas walls were rods holding cotton curtains in an African print. On the other side of the wooden wall behind our beds was an ebony vanity with two sinks, brass sconces on both sides of the mirrors, and an amenity basket holding the lodge's own brand of shampoo, conditioner, and sunscreen. An indoor toilet and shower were behind curtains. But there was also an outdoor shower, which was accessible via a wooden ramp from the tent. The shower was built into a tree stump, and totally private, with a wooden fence on one side, and foliage on the others. Although it, too, was raised off the ground, it was possible for animals to walk through the thicket below.

I could barely wait to use the outdoor shower, as I turned on the hot water, and lathered my hair—what a feeling of being one with nature. But before I knew it, the clouds covered the sun, and the breeze picked up. I dried quickly, and hustled inside the tent to dress.

It's customary to take an afternoon rest after lunch, during the heat of the day, so Shirley and I retired to our tent. Before we knew it, the wind was blowing the canvas walls until they shook the curtain rods from their pockets, and all the curtains landed on the floor. The overhead fan above our bed swung above us like a trapeze, and I could only hope that it was sufficiently secured. As the wind continued to blow, the rain came, and we were surprised to find ourselves piling on additional sweaters and long pants, and climbing beneath the comforter, even covering our heads. Meanwhile, the wind continued to blow through the tent, even though the window and door flaps were tightly secured. BANG, BOOM, CRASH! What was going on around us? We were afraid to peek from beneath the covers. We managed to fall asleep, and when time came to prepare ourselves for the afternoon game drive, we slowly climbed out from the covers. The lamps on the shelf behind the bed were now rolling around on the floor—we were lucky they didn't fall on our heads. We picked up the curtains, and slipped the rods back into their pockets. Anything that wasn't tacked down was strewn across the tent.

Linkwasha Tented Camp in Hwange, Zimbabwe was situated in the midst of the park. Each tent was hundreds of feet away from neighboring tents, and accessible only by wooden walkways. Entering from our patio, the king-sized bed was under mosquito netting. An indoor shower, toilet, and wooden vanity were to the right. The fact that there was a glass wall to watch the game through while in the bathroom didn't detract from its privacy. Walking through curtained French doors, I found the outdoor shower, built into the rocks, yet totally open to the park, where one could watch the wart hogs and Cape Buffalo around the camp, while showering.

We were informed the moment we arrived that, as we were situated within the park, the wild animals were free to roam—and they did—all around us. Using the outdoor shower at night was *not* recommended, lest we find ourselves in the presence of some "gamey" company. And under no circumstances were we to leave the main lodge for our tents without being escorted by an armed guide.

As we left camp for our afternoon game drive, a herd of Cape Buffalo (one of Africa's most deadly animals) meandered their way into the camp, and only a short distance from our tent. That evening, while I was getting ready for bed, I heard an argument outside—it sounded like elephants. As I climbed into bed, I heard a lion grumbling, and then there was a muffled encounter between the lion and another animal. The next morning, only a few hundred feet from our tent, we found the result of the previous night's encounter—a dead buffalo.

Camping out ...
Marrakech, Morocco

Some tourists have to drive all the way to the desert and its high sand dunes to camp out. We found another alternative.

First impressions are certainly important, and none more so than our encounter with our hotel. What were we to think, when we were told the elevator wasn't working and we had to carry our bags—to the third floor? "At least it's clean," I remarked to Shirley. This wasn't the first time she had heard those words, and thinking back on the hotels in Myanmar, she wasn't impressed. No, cleanliness wasn't a good equalizer anymore.

But after a long day of traveling, we were still glad to see our room, no matter how sparse, because we were anxious for some sleep. Perhaps at first we thought the room was warm, since we just climbed three flights of stairs. But it didn't take long after we turned the lights off to realize that the air-conditioner was a fixture from the past, and had long ceased operating, despite any cajoling—or threatening—from the room's occupants.

As anyone who's visited the desert knows, hot as the days may be, temperatures drop a lot at night, sometimes making it even cold. "Maybe if we open the balcony door," I suggested, "the cool night air will help us out." I climbed back into bed, after pushing the heavy door aside, and waited for the room to cool off. I was encouraged, because by now it was quite chilly on the balcony. After waiting, and waiting, and waiting, we concluded that the room wasn't about to cool off. Another idea came to mind. "You know, one time in Tunisia, we dragged our mattresses onto the balcony, and it was much cooler." Shirley readily agreed, and we helped each other pull the clumsy mattresses onto the small balcony. Our privacy needed to be addressed next, because the hotel was at the edge of the parking lot, and a big park was situated across the street. Hastily, we grabbed our bedspreads, and draped them over the railing, so no one could see us.

The cool night air felt fresh, but before long, we found ourselves buried beneath the blankets. Then there was the noise coming from the park—teenagers and children shouting, laughing, and playing as though it was mid-morning, instead of mid-night. As though that wasn't bad enough, the noise and excitement awoke all the dogs in the neighborhood, and they began barking. Then there was the traffic—always the noisy traffic.

All too soon, the alarm woke us up. Peeking out from beneath the blankets, we glanced around us and started laughing. What on earth would someone think if they saw what we had done to the room? The maid would certainly be in for a big surprise, when she entered and found the bed frames without any mattresses on them. Then, when she looked to the balcony, she'd discover them hidden amidst the pillows, sheets, and blankets. I'm sure the bedspreads, now clinging to the railings (as if to save themselves from falling three stories to the ground) would be a real attention-getter. We could only surmise what people in the parking lot or across the street in the park would think when they saw our balcony. Then again, maybe they'd feel right at home, when they saw the fort we had built.

WATCH OUT FOR "COZY" AND "CHARMING" ...
DAS CATARATAS HOTEL, IGUASSU FALLS, BRAZIL

Things aren't always what they're supposed to be ... or maybe our expectations are the real problem.

I couldn't believe our good fortune, when I heard that our tour group was staying at the famous Das Cataratas Hotel. Being the only hotel located within the Brazilian national park, the opportunity of staying in this Colonial hotel, literally located right across from the famous Iguassu Falls was a treat. The guidebooks described it as "cozy" and "charming," two words that should have tipped me off right away. But when our bus pulled up in front of the pink building at midnight, and spotlights illuminated the tower, I just knew I was staying in one of the truly stately hotels of the world.

"Stately" it was, indeed, since world figures such as President Clinton and Prime Minister Tony Blair had stayed here. We exited the bus, and the total blackness of the night engulfed us. The rush of the falls could be heard across the street. We ascended the few stairs to the portico, and entered the hotel's registration area. It was immediately apparent that the building was undergoing some renovation. But it was late, hot, and we were very tired, having flown from Santiago via San Paulo to Iguassu Falls. It was also apparent that the public areas of the hotel weren't air-conditioned, and a pungent mildew smell clung to the thick night air—but what did we expect, right across the road from the falls?

I was anxious to see our room. At least it was on the first floor, so we didn't have to walk too far. Once again, travel books described the rooms, "... spacious and well-equipped to meet the needs of any traveler, with color TV, mini-bar, central air-conditioning and heating." We weren't far from the equator, so I couldn't imagine why anyone would require heat.

I put the key card in the lock, and pushed the door open. By this time, I wasn't too surprised at what I found, twin beds without any box springs—just mattresses set on the bed boards, and quite low at that. We had an old wooden armoire, but when I opened the door, I couldn't imagine putting any clothes in it, because of the mildew smell. Tucked on the floor of the armoire were two hairy brown things, all folded up. I took them to be very heavy woolen blankets—maybe in case the heat didn't work. Could one be called "cozy" and the other "charming"? The entire room was not much larger than my walk-in closet at home, and my bed was pushed against the air-conditioner, which was set into the wall, not "central" air-conditioning, as was advertised. The only window we had was well above my head, and made of frosted glass. I assumed that this was for privacy on the first floor, even though a "peeping Tom" would have to be seven feet tall to see inside. The wooden floor was dark, and noisy. So much for a "spacious" room with amenities—I looked and looked, but still couldn't find even one amenity.

There wasn't adequate space around the bathroom sink to place one's toiletries, so I set them on the bowed toilet seat cover, only to find that when I turned my back, they rolled onto the floor, one by one. They wouldn't roll out of the bidet, but that thought wasn't too appealing.

The room was so warm when we arrived, that I immediately switched the air-conditioner into high speed. When I climbed into bed after my shower, the cold air was blowing directly on me, as the unit was only inches from my bed. I didn't want to awaken my roommate, so I fumbled in the darkness to find a blanket on the floor of the armoire. My hand touched something fuzzy, and I could only hope that it wasn't alive. No, thank goodness, it was either "cozy" or "charming", one of the blankets I had seen earlier. Heavy as it was, I buried myself beneath it, so I wouldn't catch cold. Then there were the sheets, which had a strong mildew smell.

Having taken a nasty fall in Santiago, the hard mattress wasn't kind to my bruises. Turning over under the heavy blanket drained me of nearly all my strength, and its weight put unwelcome pressure on my aching body. I was tired, but I couldn't wait for morning to arrive. In the back of my mind, I wondered what rooms "Bill" and "Tony" had occupied on their visits. I couldn't imagine the former President of the United States and the Prime Minister of Britain chasing their toiletries around the bathroom, or wrestling with a heavy, smelly brown blanket in the middle of the night—and we won't even mention those "amenities" that were awaiting all the guests!

At last—a 5-star hotel!
Dubrovnik Palace Hotel, Dubrovnik, Croatia

What qualifies as a 5-star hotel? Better yet, can a hotel really be classified 5-star, if the amenities it promises aren't delivered off-season?

"And we stayed in this fabulous 5-star hotel." During the course of our phone call, Pete went on and on about the wonderful room he had with a balcony that overlooked the Adriatic. Why, he even had a sitting room. As a man who sets high standards, I couldn't wait to see the Dubrovnik Palace Hotel. He'd been there a month earlier, and when I think of all the things that he could have prepared me for, the hotel wasn't foremost in my mind.

It was a long drive down the coast, and Shirley and I were pretty anxious to get to this fabulous hotel. Maybe we'd order room service, and dine in our sitting room, just enjoy the view of the Adriatic. We dashed into the lobby to avoid the ongoing rain that accompanied us throughout our drive. The lobby was very large, and very empty. It was also very modern, and too dull for my taste, but this *was* a 5-star hotel. We pressed on in anticipation, because we couldn't wait to get to that wonderful room Pete described. We opened the door in great anticipation, and found two double beds with little space to walk around them. The portable flat-screen TV sat on the desk, which pretty well prevented us from using it for anything else. With only one luggage rack, Shirley offered to keep her suitcase on the floor. "This is a 5-star hotel," we kept reminding ourselves.

I opened the bathroom door, and came face to face with putrid green tiled walls. I performed my usual bathroom check, and noticed that there was one bar of soap about the size of a one-and-one-half-inch Post-It note; no Kleenex; no clothesline; and the shampoo bottle was designed so the bottle couldn't be squeezed to release its contents. But *this* was a 5-star hotel.

Since we didn't have a balcony, or a sitting room, or even a view, for that matter, we decided to have a bite to eat in the dining room. Okay, so it was the end of the tourist season, which explained why only our tour group was in the dining room, and probably why the food on the buffet table looked dried up and cold. So, we ordered from the menu in this "5-star hotel." Shirley selected a tuna sandwich without Mayo (they didn't have any) on a baguette that couldn't be cut with a steak knife. It was void of lettuce, tomato, and fries—and what there was of the tuna slid out of the baguette when she bit into it. Meanwhile, I had a hamburger that was undercooked, with bacon that was undercooked, a little wet lettuce and tomato on a hard baguette—but my sandwich came with fries. Again, the burger slid out from the baguette, when I bit into it. We were very thirsty, and decided to splurge, ordering four glasses of Sprite. All this for only thirty-five dollars. But remember, after all, this *was* a 5-star hotel!

Chapter 3

Bathrooms

Can they really be called a "convenience?"

How many times have we been in dire need of a bathroom, only to be disappointed? Sometimes, nothing *is* better than anything! Bathrooms and plumbing tell a lot about a facility. This is the shortest chapter in the book—but a few stories pretty much cover it all!

LADIES, BEHIND THE AUNT HILL!
AFRICA

How lucky women are, we have three kinds of toilets—we're so special. Men don't have to worry about such things—but look at all the fun they're missing.

There are three kinds of bathrooms—or should I say toilets:

1. The "western" style—a porcelain commode, where one actually *sits* on a seat, some of which are cushioned, and some even heated (now isn't that a comforting thought).

2. The "eastern" style, which is also porcelain, but does *not* come with a toilet seat, and one does not sit, but *squats* over the porcelain hole in the ground.

3. The "African" style—which does not involve porcelain at all, does not have a toilet seat, or even a hole in the ground. It's similar to the "eastern" style, in that one squats—over the ground, the dry, dusty ground, and hopes the wind doesn't blow the dust ... well, you get the idea.

Picture this, you're on safari, and it's late morning. That coffee you had for breakfast is looking for a way out of you, and there's nothing around—except for dusty ground, scrub grass, and some trees—oh, yes, and there's a berm. All at once, the women in the vehicle head off towards the berm, unzip their pants, and squat down—all the while chatting, and warning each other to avoid the prickly weeds. But while in the midst of squatting, a man wanders over the berm. Maybe he doesn't notice the ladies (after all, he worked in the opal mines of Australia all his life—there were probably a lot of things he didn't notice).

"John!" one of the women shouts, "You're in the ladies' room!"

Flustered, John trips over his own shoelaces, and dashes back to where he came from.

On another occasion, while in Namibia, Botswana, and Zimbabwe, there were innumerable aunt hills everywhere. Morning break time would come around, and our guide would simply point and shout, "Ladies, behind the aunt hill!"

IF YOUR WAY IS SO GREAT—STAY WITH IT!
CHINA

I can take the "eastern" toilets—if I have to—cumbersome though it is, to sometimes have to undress (in the event that I'm wearing slacks or, worse yet, a scooter skirt), so you don't soil your clothes, while crouching down over the hole.

Some things are just a part of travel—bad beds, flight delays, questionable food—you just get used to them. But "eastern" toilets—noooooo, you never get used to them. Actually, I don't know why they're referred to as "eastern" toilets, because I've encountered them from Morocco to the Balkans and back. Of course, the customary "hole in the ground" is a little fancier in some places than in others. For instance, some of these "facilities" are surrounded by porcelain. Some even flush, while others have a water box overhead, with a cord to pull when you've completed your "activity." But beware of those, sometimes you have to dash out of the stall or be prepared for a shower. Now and again, there's a bucket full of water and a cup to "flush" your ... away.

Then there's the juggling of your handbag, camera bag, or just cameras dangling from around your neck. In the event that you don't have a companion willing to hold your valuables for you, it's a challenge to balance over the hole, so as not to end up with wet feet—or clothes.

What sends me into a rampage, however, is standing in line with a group of western tourists for the only "western" toilet in a restaurant in China, and having a Chinese woman exit the stall, when there were ample "eastern" toilets available for her use! Whenever women tourists complain about the "eastern" toilets, tour leaders are only too happy to point our how much cleaner they are, compared to ours (go figure?). One can only hope that now that China is getting used to western ways, they'll move full speed ahead to convert their toilets.

Chapter 4
Transportation

Getting there is half the fun!

A camel, an elephant, a plane, a taxi ... Depending on where you are in the world, you may find yourself "enjoying" one of these means of transportation. Also, depending where you are in the world, the camel or elephant may be preferable to the taxi!

IF IT'S TUESDAY, DON'T STOP AT RED LIGHTS ...
CAIRO, EGYPT, 1976

An "introduction" to Cairo? Uh, uh, no way—a taxi ride through downtown Cairo is a real baptism by fire!

I peered into the back of the taxi. The vinyl seat was covered in a layer of dust. We were on our way to the airport to see if they'd located our lost luggage. I looked down at my white pants, and wondered if I really wanted to take a seat in the vehicle, since I was wearing the only clothes that made the flight to Cairo. What choice did I have? I had to get to the airport, and one taxi was as dirty as the other. My next question was whether I should sit down and *slide* along the bench seat, with my companions trailing behind me ... or should I creep along the length of the back seat, and then *sit* down? Either way, my pants would reflect that I'd been dusting *something* off, and the taxi's back seat would be clean. I opted for the second choice, and sat down gently on the edge of the seat.

The dashboard was covered in brightly colored fake fur, and trimmed in tiny Italian lights. Meanwhile, the radio blared Middle-Eastern music. Maybe being crammed into the back seat with three other women was a good thing, because it kept us from rolling around whenever the driver took a corner on two wheels. I noticed that he wasn't stopping at any red lights. Instead, he just blasted his horn at every intersection to announce his impending arrival. When I brought this to the attention of our tour guide, and asked why the red lights went ignored, he responded that drivers didn't have to stop at red lights on Tuesdays. I wondered if they bothered to stop on any of the other six days of the week!

Not to worry, we'd be safe. I noticed an open Koran tucked away amidst the fake fur on the dashboard. Certainly, Allah would protect us now. As though the horrific traffic wasn't enough to deal with, we'd occasionally come upon a horse-drawn cart, clip-clopping its way ever so slowly through the busy Cairo streets—guess carts don't have to obey the red stoplights either—providing it was Tuesday! The tour books never mentioned all this. They just said, "Traffic in Cairo can be quite heavy at times, so visitors should take care before crossing streets." While tour books tend to overstate the immensity of buildings and monuments, the traffic situation was *always* an understatement.

Dreams and fantasies really do come true ...
Masai Mara, Kenya, 1984

When I was a little girl, my dolls were always having adventures. Sometimes, pirates captured them, or perhaps they were floating in my Easter basket—a hot-air balloon—seeking adventure.

Hot-air balloon flights were a novelty back in 1984. As a result, our guide Mohamed had to obtain special permission from the park ranger to drive through the park in the middle of the night to Keekorok Lodge, where we'd be embark on our balloon ride.

It was another long day of fresh air and good food. I retired at 10:30 PM like a lazy lion, expecting to fall fast asleep. But at approximately 11:00 PM, I tried to tell myself that the noise I was hearing outside our tent was anything but thunder. At *exactly* 11:15 PM, the rain began. For the next three hours and forty-five minutes, I stayed awake listening to what appeared to be pouring rain. When the alarm clock went off at 3:00 AM, and Geri awoke, I triumphantly announced that it had been raining continually since 11:15 PM, and I was certain that our flight would be cancelled. However, unless we dressed and walked down to the camp's reception area, where we were to meet Mohamed, we'd have no way of knowing whether we were flying or not.

The camp's watchman (for wild animals) came to meet us at 4:00 AM, and announced that our driver was already waiting for us. I was surprised to find the path outside our tent so dry, because the floor of the bathroom that was adjacent to our tent (and everything inside) was dripping wet. The thatched roof itself was depositing big droplets of water on my head, as I crossed from one side of the bathroom to the other, clutching a towel about my shoulders to avoid getting pelted by raindrops.

Mohamed packed six of us into his vehicle, and we set out across the plains in complete darkness. When the headlights went out on the rocky road, we gasped in horror at the thought that we'd be stranded in the blackness of the African night. But once more, Mohamed's competency quickly remedied the situation, and within seconds we were off again, lights brightly shining on the dark road.

Our powerful headlights illuminated the eyes of herds of wildebeest, making them look like thousands of flickering candles. Suddenly, on Mohamed's right, two lionesses appeared. They were apparently startled by our bright lights, and just as one pulled back, preparing to spring on the vehicle, he quickly veered to the left, out of her path.

It took nearly ninety minutes to cover the fifty miles between our camp, Kichwa Tembo, and Keekorok Lodge, where we'd meet our pilots, Tim and Dudley. Upon arrival, they drove us to the liftoff point. We watched in awe, as several men filled the giant balloons, which were spread flat on the ground. While the balloon was filling with hot air, several men walked inside, distributing more air into what now looked like a huge tent.

There were two balloons, one holding two to three passengers, and Dudley; and our balloon, which carried the six of us, and our pilot Tim. Like children, we scrambled around for pictures, before lifting off. At about 7:30 AM, we carefully climbed inside the basket, and were instructed about landing positions and procedures. Tim gave a giant blast of heat and bright orange flames arose overhead, filling the balloon with still more hot air.

Contrary to our expectations, we lifted off the ground so gently that we were hardly aware of any movement at all. Slowly, slowly, we climbed, and were carried away over the lodge itself. Tim was excited, because the course over Keekorok was a first-time accomplishment for him in the three months he'd been piloting in Kenya. Gently, we climbed over the cottages and beautiful swimming pool. Natives working at the lodge rushed out of their compound to wave as our giant yellow and orange balloon passed overhead.

Toward Tanzania we soared until reaching about eleven hundred feet. Up and down we drifted, still slowly, at first looking way up to our sister balloon in the distance, then peering down on her. Below us, a cheetah raced across the green plains. And there were endless herds of wildebeest playing follow-the-leader through passages below. A day earlier, the herd's leader was a lone impala. These foolish clowns of the plains followed the Pied Piper. The shadows of our balloon covered vast areas below, while wildebeest cavorted in and out of the shadows.

As our journey proceeded and time passed, the sun peeked from behind puffy white clouds ... then the blue sky pushed its way into our photos for a breathtaking picturesque back-drop behind the other balloon. The land below seemed to go on endlessly, and the hills blended into the plains; only a faint hint of the horizon distinguished the sky from the ground below. It was as if we were in a fishbowl, looking all around, peering into another world. There were no distinguishable landmarks, no wind, no cold, just a lazy floating back and forth, up and down.

After an hour and a quarter, we slowly descended, assuming crouching positions for landing, lest our basket fall on its side and drag us. Within minutes, the crew packed the balloons up and placed the baskets on the back of two trucks. Meanwhile, a champagne picnic had been prepared for us. Red-and-white checkered tablecloths were spread across the grassy plain, and we seated ourselves comfortably in a circle. The pilots began filling, and refilling, our glasses with champagne as we passed pineapple, hardboiled eggs, cold chicken, cheese, and cakes among the group.

Though the fresh air worked up our appetites, we girls nibbled at the tasty food and hungrily drank in Dudley's good looks. Perhaps I saw the movie *King Solomon's Mines* with Stewart Granger once too often, but I finally found someone who could fill Stewart's shoes. Here was a rugged Englishmen who had set forth on the "Dark Continent" in search of adventure—and fortune. Dudley was smartly dressed in his orange jumpsuit, zipped modestly to mid chest. With all the champagne we drank, it wasn't long before we were a little tipsy. We alternated sipping from our glasses to wallowing in the blue seas of his eyes, which stood out beautifully against his tan face and sandy hair. His warm smile captivated our hearts.

I've taken two more balloon flights on subsequent safaris. The picnics became more elaborate, and the prices were much higher. But there was something so special about our first flight. I never did forget Dudley, and I asked about him when I returned several years later. Sadly, he'd passed away. I don't know if he ever found his fortune, but he certainly fulfilled our dreams and fantasies (in more ways than one).

UP, UP AND AWAAAAAY ...
ACAPULCO, MEXICO, 1985

Aside from two bodies washing up on the beach after a storm, this was a pretty uneventful trip. We were walking down the beach one last time, when a young Mexican man called out, "Lady, want to parasail?"

Okay, so I'm impressionable. Day after day, all day long, they flew overhead. It was my last day, and the end of my Mexican vacation. Having watched those adventurous tourists soaring over the bay every day, the sport of parasailing looked neither difficult nor frightening.

Before I had a chance for a second thought, two young men rushed towards me with a life vest, each one hoping to zip me in. It was a tough squeeze, and it still didn't zip up very far—but the little Mexican didn't mind—he had a good time trying. I turned to my friend with instructions on how to use my movie camera. I'd no sooner finished handing it to her, than the speedboat took off for deeper water, and I ran down the beach until the parachute caught the wind and swept me over the bay. Gently, very gently, I rose higher and higher over the shimmering deep blue water. The sun sparkled on the white hotels surrounding the beach. The scenery was breathtaking. I was exhilarated.

Before long, we were heading back to the beach for landing. Following the instructions I'd been given, I pointed my toes downward. Then I saw them. Both little Mexicans were waiting to grab me by the legs, their arms outstretched—big smiles on their faces, their white teeth glistening in the sun. Ohhhhhhh, here I come! They grabbed me to slow me down—then they let go! The parachute was dragging me down the beach on my stomach—and my friend was filming away. She was certain to zoom in, just as I had showed her. My movies ended with my backside in the camera as I collected sand in my mouth.

"Good landing!" one Mexican shouted. "Yesterday, the lady broke her arm when she landed!"

No Three-Ring Circus, But a Circus Just the Same ...
Jaipur, India

What child isn't excited to see those magnificent circus elephants for the first time? There's the pageantry, the parade of elephants in their colorful blankets, and then there's the beautiful young woman in her glittering costume with plumes and feathers. She climbs on the elephant's trunk, and he gently lifts her, so she can sit behind his enormous ears. She proceeds to ride him all around the circus ring, to the applause of the audience.

I'd always wanted to ride an elephant, and the Amber Fort in Jaipur offered my first opportunity. One after another, we watched the tourists ascend a stairway to a platform, where they climbed into a rack on the back of an elephant. It wasn't as showy as nestling in the crook of his trunk to get on his back, but it was a lot safer, where tourists were involved. There wasn't any applause, but then again, we weren't required to wear any feathered headpieces.

All along the way up the paved ramp to the Fort, children played flutes, as they accompanied the elephants on their journey. And in between "fluting," they begged for rupees. No, this wasn't quite the same as in the circus, although wild monkeys could be seen frolicking on the high walls around the Fort.

~ FAST FORWARD ~

More Experienced on Elephants, We Were Ready for Anything (Well, Almost) ...
Katmandu, Nepal

Another opportunity for an elephant ride—this time, through the jungle! Shirley and I sat back to back, with our legs dangling off the sides of the elephant. However, Karen was left to ride backwards, with her legs off his rear-end, and holding on for dear life, lest she slide off and into the mud and fresh elephant droppings. Bill, lucky man that he was, ended up on another elephant altogether.

A short distance into the jungle, the path became very muddy, due to the darkness and dampness of the thick foliage. Every time an elephant lifted a foot, we could hear the "gushy" sound. The path also became elevated—and narrow, very narrow. The elephants were quite sure-footed, despite their sloshing around in the thick, wet mud. They used their trunks to determine where their next step would be, by smelling the ground before placing a foot down. There was only a small iron bar to hold onto, as the elephants continued to ascend—and descend—the winding pathway through the jungle.

When the road straightened out and widened, the elephant caretakers (mahouts) climbed off their elephants to demonstrate a few tricks. Meanwhile, an absent-minded, elderly gentlemen in our group, leaned over the side of his elephant, and his passport fell out of his pocket—right into the mud. Not only did the elephant pick up the passport, but he also handed it back to the man, along with a cloth to wipe it off!

~ FAST FORWARD ~

Who needed a mahout—we were in charge now!
Chiang Rai, Thailand

Shirley and I had barely left the elephant camp with a trainer riding behind the elephant's head, when he decided to desert us. He simply jumped off the elephant—the lead elephant in the group, nonetheless—and ran into the bushes. Meanwhile, we were left sitting in a seat on the elephant's back, with only a rope dangling loosely in front of us, tied from one end of the carrier to the other—to hold us in (yeah, right).

The elephant carried on, business as usual, while the trainer was in the bush, doing his morning "business," I assume. I'd ridden an elephant in this camp, in northern Thailand, outside of Chiang Rai a few years before. However, I didn't recall the hills being so steep. The sure-footed elephant obviously knew where he was going, with or without a trainer, so we weren't too concerned. Climbing up the hillside wasn't as frightening as the trip down, with only that skinny little rope to hang onto. But like little children, we were filled with delight, as we looked at the long line of elephants trailing behind us with other tourists clutching their ropes.

Once we covered the hillside, it was time to return to the river camp to watch the elephants being bathed. We descended the road, and entered the river. Splash, whoosh ... the elephants enjoyed the cool river water, and jostled their passengers back and forth, in anxious anticipation of their baths.

When bath time was over, the elephants entertained us with a variety of tricks, a little soccer, and even an oil-painting demonstration. The audience enjoyed the frolicking elephants and their trainers. I, meanwhile, couldn't take my eyes off the poor women who trailed around the camp in their heavy yellow rubber raincoats and black rubber boots, picking up fresh elephant dung. I didn't know which was worse—having to wear all that rubber in the heat of the tropics, or dragging buckets of fresh elephant dung around the camp. Hmmm, guess there are a lot worse jobs in the world, and that had to be one of them.

Home, home on the range ...
Mount Kenya, Africa

Yes, the words of the old cowboy song came to mind, as I mounted my mighty steed. The last time I rode a horse was in Petra, Jordan. Other than a pony ride at carnivals, the previous time was on a trip out west as a little girl. I didn't fare well on that ride, either, as the strong-minded horse took off on a gallop, and jumped a large tree stump!

Surely, this would be different. For one, I wasn't out west, so the words, "where the deer and the antelope lay (or was it play?)" had to be changed to "where the lion and wildebeest lay (or maybe it should have been "play")." In any event, we were at the Mount Kenya Safari Club, once owned in part by the late actor William Holden. It so happened that we had some time on our hands, before departing for our next stop on safari and, well, the horses were available for riding.

But these weren't just horses, they were *Arabian* horses. I don't know what made me think they would have any better manners than other horses, but I mounted one anyway. Fortunately, there was someone from the resort to lead us on our ride around the grounds. So several of my friends and I knew we'd be safe.

Anyone who has ever been to, or seen the Mount Kenya Safari Club, can't help but marvel at its stately elegance. Ladies have to wear skirts or dresses for dinner, and men have to drag a sports jacket along on safari, just for an overnight stay. Aside from the extensive African decorating, which includes doorways framed by elephant tusks, and zebra skin rugs, the grounds and lawns are fabulous. Caretakers must manicure them with a cuticle scissors, because not a weed can be found on the rolling green lawn. The resort has expansive land, and fabulous flowerbeds surround the villa accommodations, main house, swimming pool, and grounds in general.

That being said, my horse had an appetite for the flowers—all the flowers—regardless of their species. We followed the leader, and I did my best to control this hotheaded horse, however, like most males, he continued to ignore me. I held the reins firmly, but I was no match for a ton of horsemeat. We turned the corner of one of the villas on the periphery of the grounds, and the next thing I knew, my horse pulled me forward, as he grasped a mouthful of gladiolas. Chomp, chomp, chomp. I was in shock, and hoped that the leader didn't know that the black beauty I was riding just took out a day's work in plantings.

Moving on around the grounds, no flowers in sight, I was feeling I finally had a grip on things. Suddenly, black beauty found some more flowers, ripping the reins through my fingers, as he wrestled with me for more lunch. "OUCH ... oh my god!" I shouted, immediately calling the leader's attention. Now I was in trouble—he left the head of the group, and rode back to me.

"What is the matter?"

"I can't seem to control this horse ..."

"Well, you must hold the reins firmly."

"I was, only he overpowered me, and the reins ripped through my hands. Look at this, he broke my nail!"

Sympathy wasn't in the leader's vocabulary, as he looked at me with disgust. He turned his obedient horse, and proceeded to the front of the group. Meanwhile, I made up my mind that if black beauty wanted to eat every flower on the grounds, I didn't care. When next we encountered a flowerbed, I leaned forward—before he could rip my hands with the reins—and I let him eat his little heart out.

"Hope you get a stomach ache," I whispered, as he munched away.

WHAT HAS TWO WINGS AND A SMALL BODY?
OKAVANGO DELTA, BOTSWANA, 1992

Sounds like a description of Tinkerbell. One thing was for certain, this was an adventure no one would ever forget!

In answer to the question, a fly? Bug? Spider? Butterfly? Plane? Wait a minute! Just how *small* are we talking, if we're talking about a plane? Well, we're talking pretty small, like so small that you have to declare your weight *before* they let you on the plane—*and* there are only three passengers and one pilot on a five-passenger Cessna. And I'm going to fly into Botswana's Okavango Delta on this "plane"? Uh huh, you got it. And I have to declare my weight in order to get on this plane? Right again. Then think about this—there are two things most women lie about—their age and their weight! If I shave a good ten pounds or more off *my* weight whenever asked, e.g., for a driver's license, what do those who outweigh me by a hundred pounds do? You got the picture? This was perhaps more frightening than the thought of the flight itself.

Bill, Shirley, Karen, and I were packed into the plane like peanuts in a shell. I slid into the unoccupied co-pilot's seat like a greasy hamburger into a bun. Shirley and Karen squeezed into the seat behind me, followed by Bill, who was surrounded by our four duffle bags. Whoever thought twenty pounds in a duffle bag could fill the space to its boundaries, but those suckers were hard to zip closed. Yes, there were weight restrictions, and I could only hope that my friends met theirs, or we might not make it off the ground. I took one look at the ample figure of our lady bush pilot, and wondered if this chick had to declare *her* weight. If not, we'd be dumping our bags overboard before the door even closed.

Up, up, and away ... we soared from the tiny city of Maun over the Delta. I was giddy with delight, even if I couldn't hear anything but the roar of the prop engines just outside my window. When we started descending, I looked for the airport, but all I found in return was a narrow landing strip. Bump, bump, bump. We touched down on the dusty ground in the middle of nowhere. The engine gave one last whirl and a loud belch before halting. I felt like I'd been in a clothes dryer, when someone opened the tiny door from the outside. I tried to unfold my legs, and straighten my head, but before I could do so, I tumbled forward. Two strong arms caught this graceless piece of humanity, before I landed in the sand.

"Welcome to Botswana, my name is Alistair."

My eyes looked upwards towards the source of the deep voice with a pronounced English accent. The sun was beaming into my eyes, but I managed a squint. He was tall, dark, and gorgeous, with the bluest eyes I'd ever seen. I knew right then that maybe we were off to a good start after all.

THE THRILL OF IT ALL ...
KISANE TO CHOBE, SOUTHERN AFRICA, 2003

I found it particularly amusing on my first flight in the region, when the pilot pulled out a map as he was flying. Made me a little nervous to think he didn't know where we were going.

The weather was looking fine, as we flew our 5-passenger Cessna out of the Okavango Delta in Botswana. The pilot was looking pretty good as well. During our many flights in the region, we crossed paths often, and it was always nice to see a friendly, blonde-haired South African pilot. Of course, none of the pilots in the bush country looked more than sixteen years old ...

Now it was my turn to fly with the pilot Spike. Take-off from Kisane went smoothly enough, but there was an impending storm, and it promised to be in our path. I squeezed myself into my seat just above the tail of the little plane, surrounded by three women I'd met on safari. Hunched over so as not to hit my head on the ceiling, my chin was nearly resting on my knees, as I struggled to take my hand-held electronic checkers game out of my bag. Hadn't played it in years, and I was just now getting the hang of it once again.

All of a sudden, I noticed the ride getting a little bumpy. Taking my eyes off the game, I looked to my left and saw a wall of rain and storm clouds. I looked to my right, and found a mirror image. We were flying right *through* the storm. I was about to make a major play on the game board, when the plane took a huge dip, and I felt as though my seat was about to drop out from under me. Now *that* got my attention. My legs were nearly over my head, and my stomach wasn't far behind. I sobered up for a minute, and then regressed to my childhood days. The others were saying what they thought could be their last prayers, while I rode the bumps with all their rocking and rolling like a kid on a roller coaster, unable to contain my excitement.

At last we approached the runway at the airport near Chobe National Park. Elephants were on the periphery, as Spike pulled the plane to a halt, and helped us jump out, so we could make a dash for the small terminal in the downpour. A few minutes later, Spike entered the terminal. I couldn't help myself. I took one last peek over my shoulder at the young pilot. I wasn't too surprised to see that after that flight, he didn't look sixteen years old anymore. No, he looked at least nineteen now.

Chapter 5

Shopping

Woman's favorite sport!

Early on, I learned that if there's something you really want, don't think you'll find it elsewhere. On my first trip abroad, at a tender age, I learned that a small paperweight of the Coliseum in Rome was insignificant enough, but I regretted not buying one, just the same. When I returned two years later, I came home with one to spare. My motto became, "If you can't live without it, buy it now!"

Gone are the days of *little* souvenirs, however. I've shipped silk screens and porcelain tea sets from Japan, a sewing machine from Switzerland, a zebra hide from Kenya, sheepskin from New Zealand, lamps and oriental rugs from China and Kashmir, and gilded wooden statues and cabinets from Thailand. An Egyptian camel saddle and Russian balalaika have finally made their way into storage closets, and a linen tablecloth from the Netherlands was disposed of in a garage sale, still in the original package, unopened. Yes, long gone are the days of paperweights! But, come to think of it, they were a lot easier to shop for, not to mention getting them home …

MAYBE NEXT TIME WE SHOULD ASK FOR GRANDMA'S FALSE TEETH?
SRINIGAR, KASHMIR, INDIA, 1980

Bargaining is a way of life in some countries. So much so, that it's considered an insult not to participate. The problem is not letting your bargaining partner see how interested you really are.

Our plane finally cleared the heavy cloud coverage in the Annapurna Mountains that prevented us from landing in Srinigar, Kashmir, a day earlier. The tour brochures couldn't have prepared us for our stay on the beautifully carved wooden houseboats that were built for the British during the period of the Raj. They were permanently moored on the banks of Lake Dal, and transportation across and around the lake was in a small boat called a shakira. We had spent the day being rowed around the lake by one of the local men. The shakira had a canopy overhead to protect us from the sun; however, there was a chill in the mountain air, so my companion Cora and I nestled under a blanket, as we leaned against the back of the bench seat, with our legs spread out in front of us. Meanwhile, local men, women, and children rowed their one-person boats alongside ours to sell all sorts of wares, from beautiful fresh flowers to gemstones.

Later in the day, we were warming ourselves near the stove in the center of the parlor, when our guide gave us still another surprise. "After dinner, we'll have a visitor" John informed us. "It's traditional for some of the local people to stop by the houseboats to show you their wares."

"What kind of things do they sell?" I asked, my curiosity piqued, as I salivated over the thought of literally shopping in the comfort of our boat.

"Oh, mostly suede coats and furs."

Furs, did he say "furs?" I could hardly wait for dinner to end.

A short time later, we settled in the parlor, and awaited our visitor. Sure enough, there was a knock on the door, and a little Indian man appeared, laden with all sorts of treasures. I tried to hold back my interest, lest he see how anxious I was to buy some of his things. I first caught sight of a soft suede jacket, trimmed with fur down the front and around the sleeves. The diamond-cut suede pieces were embroidered in the traditional Kashmiri design. Then I focussed on a spotted fur jacket. The shading and coloring of the fur was very subtle in soft gold and beige, and was dotted with spots.

"What kind of fur is this?" I asked.

"That's spotted Indian lynx. It comes from the Annapurna Mountains surrounding us."

Well, I just knew I had to have the fur jacket, but it was a little tight. I pulled John into the other room, and told him that I was interested in both the suede and fur jackets, but I wasn't sure how to bargain for them, especially since the fur jacket needed an extra pelt added under each arm.

"I don't know what to tell you, just pick a fair price you'd be willing to pay, and drop down. That way, it will give him a little room to bargain."

"How much you offer me?" the Indian man asked.

"I don't know," I hesitated. "This fur jacket is nice, but I'm afraid it doesn't fit."

"No problem, we fix that."

"Well, I don't really know …" I could see that he was getting anxious. "How about three hundred dollars?"

"No, that's too low, I need at least four hundred." he shot back.

"That's too much, how about three twenty-five?" I counter offered.

He proposed another counter offer, so I pretended not to be interested. "What about the fur jacket?" he asked again.

"Oh, I don't know if I want it that much, how about thirty-five for the suede jacket?" Now it was his turn to pretend to be disinterested. It was getting late, and he wanted to make a sale.

"You don't want the fur jacket? We can make it bigger" he desperately proposed one last time.

"I'll give you three seventy-five for both jackets, and that's my final offer." Reluctantly, he agreed. "And, you'll make the fur jacket bigger?"

"Okay, okay," he concurred, "it's a deal. Tomorrow I'll bring the fur jacket back, after we have made it bigger."

John closed the door behind the little man and looked at me.

"I thought you said you didn't know how to bargain," he grinned at me.

"Well, I was a little out of practice," I defended myself.

"Out of practice, you stole everything but his grandmother's false teeth!"

How'd You Do That? It Was Just a Little Magic ...
Lake Naivasha, Kenya, 1982

Be it in the bush country of Africa, or right at home, "magic" is in the eye of the beholder.

Sometimes, the things we take for granted are very special to others. Isabel and I had barely checked into our safari lodge overlooking Lake Naivasha, and I was ready to go exploring. Leaving her in the room to freshen up for dinner, I found a souvenir shop on the premises. There weren't many tourists inside, so the young men attending the shop were particularly interested in making a sale. Only they didn't expect money—they pressed me to trade them something. Trade? What did I have to offer that would be interesting enough to entice them into a deal for the Masai engagement necklaces I wanted? Then I had a fantastic idea.

"How would you like a picture of yourself?" I asked, proud of my suggestion. They were all very puzzled. How could I give them a picture of themselves right now? I pulled my Polaroid camera from my bag, and took a picture. When I showed it to the young man behind the counter, he was very excited. All his friends gathered around him, pressing against each other, looking over their friends' shoulders to see the picture. They looked at me in awe, as though I had just performed some magic. Back in those days, I'm sure none of them had ever seen themselves in a photo. My "trade" was a big hit, for sure. I walked away with two small soapstone figures of a hippo and a rhino, and paid a fair price for the necklaces. But just seeing the amazed expressions on their faces was reward enough for me.

At the conclusion of our safari, we returned to Nairobi and promptly headed to the straw market, where I fell in love with the cowhide drums that served as tables. I'd seen the same sort at the famous Mt. Kenya Safari Club (formerly owned in part by the late actor William Holden), and I could imagine one in my den, on top of my zebra hide. But I realized that there wasn't enough time to arrange for shipping, so I reluctantly tore myself away.

More than twenty-fours later, when we arrived home, I was glancing through my mail, and found a flyer from Pier One Imports. I was surprised to find a picture of a large black-and-white cowhide drum from Africa! With the discount coupon, the cost was about the same as the one I would have had to ship from Nairobi. Not wasting a minute to change clothes, I dashed off to make my purchase. Totally exhausted, I managed to drag it upstairs, and after I centered it in the middle of my zebra, I gave Isabel a call. She lived a few doors down the hall, so I asked her to come to my apartment right away—I had something to show her. When she walked through the door to the den and saw the drum, her hair almost stood straight up on her head in surprise.

"How'd you do that? I was with you every minute!"

With a wicked grin, I answered, "It was just a little magic ..."

TAKE HOME A SOUVENIR FROM THE PAST ...
CAIRO, EGYPT, 1983

In 1983, Egypt wasn't known for its perfume—France was, but not Egypt. Then again, Cleopatra had her eye shadow and perfume, though that was a loooooooong time ago.

We were on the outskirts of Cairo, in a tourist trap for certain. But jetlag still prevailed, and we were happy to have a seat, a cold Coke, and some shade. Once all the tour groups were assembled in what looked like a tent, the show began.

When the salesman spoke, I noticed that his suit was a little snug for his portly physique. He seemed to focus his attention on our tour group, and I was sitting only a few feet away from him. He informed us about the many fragrant flowers that grow in Egypt, making it very desirable for the producers of perfume. "From the time of Cleopatra, Egypt was known for it's varied fragrances." When he made this pronouncement, he puffed up his chest in pride, as if displaying medals won in battle. However, after a closer look, I noticed that the only things he displayed on his white suit were spots that didn't come out in the laundry. As a matter of fact, judging from the creases in his trousers, and the crispness of his suit jacket, I knew those spots were well pressed into the fabric over a period of time.

Holding up a plain glass bottle, he demonstrated how, after mixing the fragrance of choice, a label was affixed to the bottle. I took a hard look at the label. It was a drawing of Cleopatra, and looked as though the artist was five years old. Certainly, with all her cosmetics and fragrances, Cleo must have been better looking than this! She had a hawk-nose, and her eyes looked crossed. As the demonstration proceeded, I found it exceedingly more difficult to contain my urge to laugh.

"And, ladies and gentlemen," the salesman said most sincerely, "if you would prefer a jeweled perfume bottle, we also have those for sale." He walked over to the dusty mirrored shelf, and picked up one of the "jeweled" bottles. I knew at first glance that this was the going to be the straw that broke *this* camel's back. The jewels were nothing more than plastic beads glued on a plain bottle in hideous colors. They didn't sparkle—they didn't twinkle. Their colors fought with each other for attention, and the designs ... well, there *weren't* really any designs. When we were informed that we could purchase the jeweled bottles at a special price of thirty-five dollars each, I felt faint—and I knew it wasn't from the heat building up inside the tent.

"If you don't want to take your perfume with you, we can ship it to you—anywhere in America." He pointed to wooden boxes stacked in front of the audience, with addresses written in big black marker, "Lombard, Illinois, Chicago, Illinois, Los Angeles, California." There were destinations from all over the USA. Then I noticed something strange—none of the addresses had zip codes. Any company doing business with people from the United States or, for that matter, anywhere in the world, would know how important zip codes are in getting mail to its destination … The salesman carried on, informing everyone about how Marshall Field's, one of Chicago's best-known department stores, buys their perfume from his company. Of course, it was pointed out that Marshall Field's rebottles the perfume, and puts their label on it, not to mention raising the price. I was certain that if I'd fallen for that line, I could be convinced that the papyrus painting I bought when I entered the tent was an ancient treasure.

When the speech was finished, we sat in silence. The entire tent was quiet, very, very quiet. I would imagine that the presentation was as overwhelming for everyone there, as it was for me. The only difference is that way back at the beginning of the presentation, I was trying desperately to control my laughter. I pursed my lips to prevent little giggles from escaping, but wasn't very successful. Before long, I felt as though my head was a pressure cooker, as tears of laughter swelled in my eyes before rolling down my cheeks. I tried to keep from snorting and choking, as I muffled my giggles. It must have appeared to anyone around me that I was having a seizure. The chuckles became contagious, and my travel companions on either side of me found themselves in the same predicament of holding the gales of laughter inside.

Americans are suckers—big suckers. We have it written all over our foreheads, "*sucker.*" When put in an uncomfortable position, we can't resist a hard sell, and we give in. I knew that once someone broke under the pressure, the dam would burst, and the Americans in the room would be waving their dollars high above their heads to place an order. Instead of taking advantage of the first sucker who dug into his pockets for a greenback, and considered him or herself lucky to be off the hook, others followed along, like lemmings.

The staff couldn't work fast enough, slapping labels on bottles, taking twenty-dollar bills, and promoting jeweled bottles. I just sat in my seat and looked around me, thinking to myself, "Here I am, in Cairo, Egypt. This is a dream come true." Then I glanced about the tent. "I'm sitting in this tent, listening to a push to buy, of all things, Egyptian *perfume*."

Fast-forward to the end of the week. We were waiting for our tour bus to pick us up in front of the hotel in Luxor, and I smelled something very pungent behind me.

"What is that *smell*?" I asked, turning around, and coming face-to-face with one of the elderly men on my tour.

"I'm afraid that's me," he responded somewhat sheepishly. "My wife bought a bottle of that Egyptian perfume back in Cairo, and some of it escaped from beneath the bottle cap on our flight to Luxor, and got all over our clothes."

I looked at him a little closer. Sure enough, "*sucker*" was written all over his bald head. The temptation to laugh was overwhelming, but somehow I managed not to—but just this one time.

SUCH A DEAL ...
JERUSALEM, ISRAEL, 1983

I always promised myself that if I returned to Israel, I would buy myself an olive wood manger, like the one I bought for my sister in 1976. But it was the last few days of my trip to Egypt and Israel and, I'm afraid I was tipping a bit too generously (no doubt due to bad math calculations). By the time I arrived in Jerusalem, my wallet was looking mighty thin. But nothing ventured, nothing gained. Who knows what I might find in the old walled city. After all, bargaining was the name of the game in the Middle East. I might be able to find a manger I could afford after all.

The thrill of just being in the old walled city of Jerusalem was almost too much to bear. I walked down the Via Dolorosa (the way of the cross), and passed the Church of the Holy Sepulcher that we visited the previous day.

Shopkeepers displayed many of their wares outside their tiny shops, and pleaded for tourists to come inside. The city was colorful, alive, and bustling. But I had to stay focused, as I walked in circles, down quiet alleys, and past noisy cafes blaring Middle-Eastern music. The pressure was on, and I set myself on a course through the old city, pricing various manger sets from shop to shop, and haggling along the way. A shopkeeper saw me eyeing his manger through the glass, and he stepped to the doorway.

"Ah," he said, scratching his beard, "you are interested in the olive wood manger? I make a good deal for you."

"No deal would be good enough for me," I replied, "I can't afford it."

"How much you offer?" he asked.

"You don't understand, I hardly have any money left, I don't have a credit card, and I'm leaving tomorrow."

"Come inside," he insisted, ignoring my protests. He began wrapping the wooden figures and placing them inside the box containing the manger.

"You don't understand," I insisted again, "I don't have enough money to pay you, no matter how good your deal is."

"But you don't have to pay me now. When you get home to America, you can send me a check for thirty-five dollars." I was amazed, and tried to protest again. He would not hear of it. "I'm a Palestinian" he said, "a Christian. And I would like you to have this manger."

After I arrived home, I sent him the check with a letter thanking him for his kindness. The check was never cashed ... the letter never returned. Every time I look at my manger, I think of that kind Palestinian man. Then I look closely at the figures, and notice one Virgin Mary, one baby Jesus, two Wise Men, and *two* St. Joseph's! And then ... I chuckle.

SOPHIA, YOU HAVE COMPETITION!
ISTANBUL, TURKEY

Never in my life had I received so much attention. Shopping in Istanbul was a real challenge. Then again, I had a brief opportunity to feel like a celebrity.

I'd read about it. I'd heard about it. There were thousands of shops under one roof—which sounded better than the outlet malls scattered across America. I walked through the tall archway that led to Istanbul's Grand Bazaar, and my heart skipped a beat. Gold, gold, gold. Everywhere I looked, gold jewelry beckoned for my attention. And then there were the rugs, and leather. Leather? Skip the gold-braided caftans, and find your way to the leather clothes. Coats, jackets, skirts, all soft as a baby's behind, and just waiting for me to begin the bargaining with the all-too-anxious shopkeeper.

"Shop" is a very loose term for the thousands of stalls that lined the walkways under the roof of the Grand Bazaar. As though the maze of dirt-packed walkways wasn't bad enough, the beautiful wares for sale were distracting in themselves. And then there were the shopkeepers, whose calls to "Lady, come see my leather—I make you a good price—best price of the day, because you are so beautiful." Well, I ask you, what woman could concentrate? Obviously, these were men of good taste. WRONG! They were men of great curiosity, bad taste, and no manners, especially when it came to how to treat a lady.

In most cases, the shops were so small that by the time the customer stepped *inside*, the proprietor had to step *outside*. In this particular instance, I was interested in a leather suit but, as always, I knew I had to try it on. Looking around me, I couldn't imagine how that could be accomplished. "Of course, you may try it on," the salesman urged. Surely, he was kidding. I was pressed in by two walls of leather jackets and skirts, with barely enough room for me to stand in between—and this was the whole shop! "See ..." he said, pulling a curtain suspended from a track on the ceiling all around me. I felt like a mummy, wrapped in all this fabric, but I did so want the suit. As I prepared to remove my dress, I noticed a pair of dark eyes in the corner of the mirror. That rascal! He positioned himself so he could see through a crack in the curtain to catch sight of me in the mirror. Brusquely, I pulled the curtain closed, nearly tearing it from the track.

At another shop, I was led to a back room to try on some garments. When I flipped the light switch and turned around, the walls were covered with magazine pictures of sexy belly dancers. I looked at the merchandise in my hand, and debated over how much I really wanted the clothes. Something made me think that there could be an eye (or two) peering through a belly button in one of the photos, watching me undress. I tried to turn my back on the walls with the most pictures, as I pulled the clothes over my head.

In still another shop, a little boy took me up narrow stairs. It seemed safe—no photos of belly dancers in the little room. I started to slip my dress off, and saw two eyes peeking around the corner of the open doorway. Buttoning my dress, I stepped outside the room. "Go away, go away!" I shouted. The youngster scampered down the winding staircase, nearly tumbling head over heels.

Exhausted and disappointed at not finding what I was looking for, I started strolling down the street from the Bazaar. Suddenly, I saw a rack of leather clothes standing on the sidewalk and, as one would expect, I found precisely what I wanted. But where was the proprietor? Where could I try them on?

"You like my merchandise?" The man appeared from nowhere.

"Yes, it's very nice," I answered.

"I make you a good price."

"Well, I can't buy anything without trying it on," I hesitated.

"No problem. Come, follow me."

Where had I heard those words before? Where was he taking me? We walked down the block, and into an empty building. Workmen were remodeling the store.

"Wait a minute, what's going on?" I asked nervously.

"You want to try this on, right?"

"Yes, but ..."

"You go upstairs," he said, pointing to the winding staircase, flanked by mirrored walls.

"No one will bother me?" I asked.

"I will wait down here," he assured me—notice, he said, "*I* will wait down here."

Hesitating, I walked up the winding staircase, and the workmen were oblivious to my presence. I was getting smarter by this time, so I slid the leather skirt on *under* my dress first. I was just about to slip my dress over my head, when I looked beyond the partial wall, and saw an old man at the top of the staircase, staring straight at me.

"Get out! Get out!" I shouted, almost afraid the poor guy would fall down the stairs as he ran away. There was no mirror upstairs, so I reluctantly descended the winding staircase in the leather outfit. Halfway down, one of the workmen eyed my red hair and shouted, "Sophia Loren!" The men all dropped what they were doing to get a glimpse of me. Stunned, I stopped in my tracks, took a quick glimpse in the mirrored wall, and ran up the staircase. I never dressed so quickly in all my life—still surprised that I didn't put my dress on backwards! Uneasy, as I passed by the workmen, I made a quick retreat, depositing the leather garments in the proprietor's lap, as I ran out of the shop.

No, I didn't buy anything that day, but I did have a little hint of what it must feel like to be thought of as a celebrity.

Some women are suckers for men— me, I'm just a sucker for a bargain!
Bangkok, Thailand, 2000

Even experienced travelers do stupid things—and when a bargain is in store, I'm at the head of the class.

"Are you staying at the Holiday Inn?" The attractive young Thai woman asked, as my friend Maureen and I were waiting for the stoplight to change.

"Yes we are," I answered.

"I thought I recognized you in the lobby. I work at the registration desk. Are you interested in buying handicrafts?"

When we replied in the affirmative, she asked if we knew about the crafts market.

"They have all kinds of wonderful Thai crafts—silk, clothes, jewelry. And they are having a sale right now, but it ends at noon." Did she say, "jewelry?" "If you hurry, you can still get in on the bargains," she urged. Did she say, "bargains?"

"Well, okay, where is it?" I asked.

"Don't worry, I'll get a taxi for you." Waving down a taxi, she directed the driver in Thai, and before we knew it, we were heading in the opposite direction from where we had intended to shop. Oh well, we could always shop in our neighborhood. As the taxi maneuvered its way through the horrendous traffic to the other side of the city, we kept commenting about how friendly and helpful the woman from the hotel had been, and how lucky we were to have run into her.

The cab pulled up in front of a large building, and the doorman showed us inside. The first floor was nothing but jewelry, and after making a few price inquiries, we wondered where the bargains were. The second floor displayed a lovely variety of silk fabrics and clothes, as she had promised; but once again, where were those bargains? Disappointed, we left the store empty-handed and walked outside, expecting to climb into a taxi. But none of the drivers would take us back to our hotel. We felt like we were being held hostage, until we made a purchase. Eventually, at our insistence, one of the taxi drivers relented, and told us to climb inside. I felt like such a sucker, being set up by one of the hotel employees—*if* she really was an employee.

~ FAST FORWARD ~

STRIKE ONE ... STRIKE TWO ... NO THIRD STRIKE FOR ME!
BANGKOK, THAILAND, 2001

Sometimes, it's hard to break a bad habit. Listening to my heart, instead of my head, often gets me into trouble.

I didn't expect to find myself back in Bangkok a second year in a row. Shirley and I left the Holiday Inn and, as we were waiting for the stoplight to change, a well-dressed young Thai woman spoke to us.

"Are you staying at the Holiday Inn?" she asked. We responded that we were.

"Have you been to Bangkok before?"

"Yes," I answered, as a matter of fact, I was here last year—at the same hotel."

"Oh, then you must be familiar with the craft market. They're having a big sale right now. If you hurry, you can take advantage of some real bargains."

Maybe it was jet lag; maybe it was greed. I don't know what made me fall for it, but before long, Shirley and I were entering the back seat of the taxi that she hailed. The car immediately turned around taking us in the opposite direction. Perhaps the abrupt turn shook something into place in my head because, almost at once, I had *déjà vu*. By the time we pulled up in front of the office building, I knew I had been taken—again.

"Oh no!" I looked sheepishly at Shirley, "You'll never believe this ..."

So Carter discovered King Tut's tomb— I had my own discoveries ...
Bangkok, Thailand, 2001

Now I knew how Howard Carter must have felt when he discovered King Tut's tomb and its many treasures. "What do you see, Howard?" he was asked. "Things, wonderful things!"

I, too, saw wonderful things ... beautiful carved wooden cabinets that were gilded, and highlighted with tiny silver mirrors. Petals of lotus flowers were carved on the sides, and doors were adorned with tiny round green-and-white mirrors that twinkled ever so subtly in the shop's bright lights. Every remaining piece of wood on the cabinet was filled with tiny, meticulous carvings. All the objects before me were masterpieces.

It was my fourth trip to Bangkok, and long before my departure from home, I knew I was going to purchase such a cabinet this time. The price was always a bargain, but I couldn't find a shop willing to handle the shipping. The thought of clearing customs and the paperwork involved was also too intimidating.

"May I help you?" That's all the young sales woman had to ask.

"Do you ship your goods overseas?"

"Regularly," she responded, assuring me with her confidence.

I'd heard all I needed to; the hunt for my treasure was on. We explored the shop for a cabinet just the right size. She waylaid my concern about shipping heavy wooden objects, by informing me that all shipments were assessed by the *size* of their container, *not* their weight. The minimum size crate was much larger than the small cabinet I had selected. Then she uttered words that were music to my ears.

"You can fill it with anything that fits into the remaining space."

"For the same price?"

"For the same price." Now we were talking! Which of the shop's other treasures would find their home in America?

"The chest needs something on it ... something like ... a Buddha." I mumbled. Crawling over other furniture, cabinets, benches, and the like, I tried one Buddha after another, like hats, until I found one just the right size. Sitting in the lotus position he, too, was gilded, with an occasional tiny mirror adorning his robe. All of a sudden, that old Beatle song "I Saw Her Standing There" came to mind. Standing on a black foot-high base, the graceful statue of a woman was six feet tall. Her hands were folded in front of her chest, as if in prayer. This, however, was the Thai gesture for their welcome greeting, "sawadee kah." She was also gilded from head to toe, and dressed in a fashionable Thai-style sarong. Intricately carved, and beset with tiny red, green, blue, and silver mirrors, the sarong clung to her shapely figure. The only painting on her face was her eyes, and had her features not been Asian, and her hair not swept back and piled high atop her head, one could have mistaken her for the beautiful, exotic, and shapely Cleopatra.

One glance, and I knew she was to be mine. Of course, there would be additional dock and warehouse charges, but at a little over seven hundred dollars for the cabinet, Buddha, *and* "Sawadee" lady (including crating and shipping), these objects were a great bargain over prices in the States. I knew they would look like a million dollars amidst my other Asian furnishings.

Within a few weeks, I received word that my purchases arrived in Chicago, and headed off to the warehouse to retrieve them.

Two big men uncrated my goods at the warehouse. The cabinet and Buddha were wrapped in corrugated paper, but not the lady. The wrappings around her weren't given the same care as an Egyptian mummy, but the end result was the same. She lay on her back, gazing up at the two men. Her arms were folded in front of her, and her sarong glittered in the warehouse lights. Like Howard Carter gazing at the burial mask of King Tut, they were in awe.

"Holy cow!" one of them exclaimed.

"What do you think of her?" I asked.

"She's somethin'. Really beautiful—reminds me of my wife."

"If your wife is that pretty, you'd better hang onto her," I replied.

We covered her carefully in bubble wrap and plastic garment bags to protect her gilt and mirrors. Then they gently placed her in the trunk of my Monte Carlo. Even setting her in at an angle, between the back seats, which folded down, her feet and pedestal stuck out of the trunk. Every bump and pothole on the long ride home caused her to thump on my bumper. I couldn't help but wonder what all the cars caught in rush-hour traffic must have thought.

Once in the garage at home, I brought a dolly over to slide her onto for transport to my apartment. Grabbing her by the base, I pulled, and pulled, and pulled. Looking at the rough wood on the bottom of the statue, it was clear that though she may be shapely and delicate, this babe weighed upwards of hundreds of pounds. She was solid—solid wood. Fortunately, my neighbor's six-foot-four son came to my rescue, lifting her carefully from the trunk onto the dolly.

Inside my apartment, we placed her in a space where everyone was certain to see her, and we began the tedious work of removing yards of bubble wrap and plastic garment bags. Around and around, the bubble wrap revealed my lady. Finally, she stood there, a warm smile on her mouth, one knee gently bent, her hands clasped in greeting.

"What do you think?" I asked, a little unfairly. After all, what *could* he think? Swallowing hard, he muttered, "She something, *really* something."

~ FAST FORWARD ~

If you want it done right—find a woman!
Bangkok, Thailand, 2004

Guys drive trucks. Guys love trucks. Doesn't every guy own a truck? Apparently, they don't.

Here I was, back in my favorite shopping city. I could hardly sleep for weeks just thinking about returning for more Thai "treasures." This time, I was looking for a larger cabinet—and carved, gilded frames for the back wall of my living room alcove—oh yes, and I wanted a larger treasure chest, trimmed with those colorful little mirrors.

I was feeling pretty experienced, after having shipped my "Sawadee lady" and other wooden pieces a few years earlier. Returning to my favorite store, I began describing the types of carved wooden goods that I had in mind. To my surprise, even if I didn't see it in the store, nothing I asked for was a problem to obtain. "You want a gilded frame without little mirrors? No problem." "You want little green mirrors on the lotus flowers? No problem." I'm sure Shirley thought I was getting a little carried away, but I had visualized these beautiful things in my home for so long—and what the heck, what's one more thing?

Several weeks later, I received word about the arrival of my shipment. The warehouse wasn't near the airport like last time—better still, it was closer to home. And I was smarter now; I'd taken the measurements of the gilded wooden cabinet, and was certain I could manage it in my two-door Toyota Solara. Shirley offered to accompany me to the warehouse in her four-door Lexus—just in case. Certainly, it would fit into one of our cars—perhaps the back seat of hers might be easier.

The bad news about the warehouse was that it closed early. We drove down the expressway at top speed (and then some), and exited where we'd been told. The warehouse was in a large industrial park. We drove around, and around, and around. For forty-five minutes, we drove in circles, but couldn't find the warehouse. Finally, we came upon a UPS delivery truck—bingo! UPS drivers know their way around the whole country, don't they? Apparently, his day was going as poorly as mine, because he was lost as well. But the street we were seeking sounded familiar, and he told us we were in the wrong industrial park—we needed to be on the north side of the expressway. Glancing at my watch, I could only pray that the warehouse wasn't closing any earlier—we were down to fifteen minutes! Shirley and I nearly drag-raced down the main thoroughfare of the even larger industrial park. Then we separated—she turned one way, I was heading in another. My last hope was that one of us would reach our destination before they locked the door.

I pulled up to the office, and was told that Shirley was around back at the loading docks. Excited and exhausted, I jumped out of my car—and locked the door—with my keys in the ignition! Ouch! Besides feeling really stupid around all the young male dockworkers, I now had another problem to deal with. To their credit, the young men were ready and willing to assist me. While one tried to pry open the window, another was uncrating my goods. Dear me, that cabinet was wider than I remembered—at least at the bottom. It was almost like a pyramid, narrower at the top and wider at the bottom. Well, they pushed and pulled, and pushed and pulled, but there was no way that sucker was going into Shirley's trunk *or* her back seat. I knew I should have checked on renting a van to transport my wares home.

I was offering fifty dollars to anyone who could get their hands on a van, and follow me home with my treasures. But what kind of guys were they anyway—none of them had access to a truck or SUV? Then I heard this gruff-sounding man with a beard saying his wife was on her way over in her van with a lo-jack to open my window. Did he say van? *Her* van? Things were starting to turn around at last.

No sooner had the woman pulled onto the dock area, than I asked her if she wanted to make fifty dollars by driving the goods to my home, about twenty minutes away. *She* loaded the wooden pieces into the back of her van, as her husband managed to open my window and unlock the door. I tipped the dockhands for their hard work, and off we were. She delivered everything right to my doorstep, and unloaded the van. I guess that if you want something done—much less done right, and without a lot of fanfare, you have to cut right to the chase—and find a woman. Still can't believe none of those guys owned a truck or a van ...

TWO SHIRTS, A WATCH, AND THIRTEEN BUCKS ...
VICTORIA FALLS, ZIMBABWE

The last time I was in Vic Falls, a young woman wanted my dirty yellow canvas shoes—right off my feet. This time, I came armed to bargain with a bag full of t-shirts and watches.

Now what's a woman to do, when she's traveled over twenty hours to get to her destination? Take a shower, change clothes, and go shopping, of course! Shirley and I were back on track. When we returned to Vic Falls from our Botswana safari in 1992, the town was booming with tourists—European tourists. After a few minutes, it was enough to make us wish we were back in the bush, where we'd take our chances with the wild animals. But once again, the country was in political turmoil, and many tour operators were avoiding it. Bad for Victoria Falls, but very good for us. We were a premium—tourists willing to spend money or, better yet, trade goods for souvenirs. We headed down to the handicraft market to see if there was anything we missed the last time.

Our first stop was the indoor market operated by the local women. We strolled down the center aisle, browsing at the many hand-carved wooden objects. A beautiful wooden basket caught my eye. It was carved through to the inside, displaying Africa's many animals around the outside and on the lid.

"Lady, you like my basket?" the African woman asked.

"Very nice ..."

"How much you offer? I make you a good price." She persisted.

"How about trading something?"

"What you want to trade?"

"How about this shirt?" I reached into my duffel bag to pull out a long-sleeved Oxford shirt that had never been worn. "See the picture (logo) embroidered on the shirt? I have a watch with the same picture ..." She hesitated a little, and asked for thirty dollars in cash as well. "No, that's too much. How about another different shirt with the same picture—and thirteen dollars?" This time, I pulled out a tangerine polo shirt.

"It's a deal." She said, taking my wares out of my hands, as she gave me the wooden basket in a plastic bag.

Mission accomplished, now to the outdoor market. The young local men were all very polite, and desperate for a sale. They'd bargain for anything we'd offer them—t-shirts, watches, and even Shirley's brand-new golf socks, which she was wearing for the first time. She found somewhere to sit down, and began removing her socks for a trade. There were so many beautiful carved statues, tables, chairs—oh, oh, there it was, one of those crazy wooden chairs on three legs with a small seat (like I would sit on it anyway), and a tall back, with animals carved into it. Even if I didn't intend to use it as a chair at home, I made the mistake of trying it out. That was my downfall. The seller knew I was interested.

"Lady, only one hundred and twenty dollars."

He followed me throughout the market, begging me to buy his chair. I knew the moment I set eyes on it, that I'd find a place for it in my den, among the African décor. We were wearing each other down—his persistence, and my pretending to ignore him. Finally, I drew one of many remaining t-shirts from my duffel bag. The minute he saw the parrot sitting among the brightly colored foliage on the white shirt, his eyes got very big. He wanted to see it closer, so I handed it to him, and stepped aside for a minute to set my soda bottle down. When I turned around, he was wearing the shirt. I knew there was no turning back now—he wanted the shirt.

"OK," I said, "you can have the shirt, this watch, and sixty dollars—and that's my last offer."

"You rob me," he played on my sympathy. I knew he really liked the shirt.

"Okay, the chair is yours." He said reluctantly.

"But before we trade, how do I get it back to America?" (At last, I was getting practical.)

"There," he said, pointing to a makeshift booth. He disassembled the chair into three pieces (back, seat, and legs), and walked me over to the booth.

A Pak-Mail or UPS office it wasn't, but I certainly had to hand it to these fellows for their ingenuity. They collected every cardboard box, piece of paper (which they shredded), string, rope, and tape in the town. For eight dollars, they wrapped my chair, basket, and a few other objects into one tidy, but cumbersome, package. Now, my problem was getting the stack of heavy wooden objects back to our lodge a few blocks away. No problem, there were plenty of local youngsters who were only too happy to have something to do for a tip, so a few rushed over to us to offer their services. When we arrived back at our lodge, I asked if they would prefer a t-shirt from my bag, or two dollars.

"Can we see the shirts?"

I pulled out two outrageous shirts (souvenirs of past vacations, which were still sealed in their plastic bags). Selecting the more colorful of the two, the young man left happy, with his "I shopped Hong Kong" shirt hanging over his arm.

Chapter 6
Weather

A traveler's best friend—or worst enemy!

Weather can make or break a trip. Oddly enough, sometimes, it's the bad weather that makes a trip one you'll never forget. Doesn't everyone love a blue sky and sunny day ... but other than leaving you with lovely photos, what else can be said? It's the unexpected weather that has often left a lasting impression ...

Beware of "Light Afternoon Showers"...
Acapulco, Mexico, 1969

We arrived at the bullring at four o'clock. By five o'clock, it was still raining. At six o'clock, we accepted the obvious reality that there wasn't going to be a bullfight that afternoon.

The guidebooks said that June was the rainy season in Mexico, but that it only rained heavily for about twenty minutes in the late afternoon. We figured that by five o'clock the sunshine would be back out, and the bullfight could commence. WRONG! So, like everyone else, we left the bullring. It was mayhem outside, and taxis were precious few. I don't know what made me think it, but I managed to convince my friends that the car across the street was one of the "unmarked taxis" that I'd read about. We dashed over to it, and in English, asked the driver if his car was a taxi. He nodded in the affirmative, so the four of us climbed in. But before we could close the door, four Mexican men piled in on top of our laps. My friend Angel started screaming at them to get off of her sunburned legs, but it wasn't until I began hitting them with my closed umbrella that they finally got the idea.

Stumbling from the car, we concluded that the only way to get back to the Hilton was to begin walking—maybe when we were far enough away from the bullring, we'd get lucky, and find a *real* taxi. The bullring was located in the hills overlooking the downtown area of Acapulco, so we had a steep walk downhill. To make matters worse, we were nearly knee-deep in the dirty rushing waters. Angel chastised me, as I struggled to hold onto my umbrella to keep my hair dry. Meanwhile, the dye from the black scarf she had tied over her blond hair had begun to run. It was hard to keep from laughing, because she looked like she had a big crack across her face. My sister had already lost one of her sandals in the rushing water, and it was difficult for us to keep our balance, so we resorted to making a human link, holding onto each other as we stumbled down the hillside's flooded streets.

Eventually, we made our way down to the city, where we tried to find a taxi, or even flag down a passerby to ask for a lift. The little pink-and-white striped jeeps from the Las Brisas resort whisked past us tooting their horns. Trucks full of Mexican workers whistled at my sister as they passed us by. Her orange sundress had so much fabric that the weight of the water caused it to become nearly transparent, and it was beginning to pull off her shoulders. Finally, a car stopped, and we asked for a lift back to the Hilton.

Walking into the hotel's lobby, we were greeted by a sign that read, "No wet bathing suits allowed." We wondered if dripping clothes might be an exception. Looking like seaweed that just washed up on the beach, we were embarrassed by the other guests who were beginning to assemble in the lobby for dinner. The women were beautifully coifed, and dressed in their finery, with lots of sparkling jewelry. They were oblivious to the afternoon's treacherous downpour. Glad to be back safely after hours of slipping and sliding through the muddy water, we decided to order room service—four hamburgers and a bottle of wine!

On a walk the following morning, we wondered if this was the same city as the day before. The streets were dry and dusty, and it looked like the buildings hadn't seen rain in a year!

~ FAST FORWARD ~

PAY MORE ATTENTION TO THOSE GUIDEBOOKS— THREE STRIKES AND YOU'RE OUT!
ACAPULCO, MEXICO, 1985

Here it was, the rainy season in Acapulco, and I was back for an encore performance. Some people never learn their lesson, and I guess I'm one of them.

We were dressing for dinner, when all the electricity suddenly went out. It had been raining most of the afternoon, and when the rain and lightening stopped, we walked out on the balcony to see the extent of the power outage. All the lights were out as far as we could see, and we noticed that there were many stalled cars on the boulevard in front of our hotel. The water was collecting in the streets, and couldn't make its way over or around the grassy berms on the boulevard quickly enough, so flooding was the natural outcome. We watched as some people evacuated their cars, and climbed to the berms, while their cars filled with water.

Little by little, the lights in the hotels began blinking on, and electrical service was gradually being restored. We wisely decided not to venture downstairs for dinner, in the event that the elevators stopped operating again. The following morning, the newspaper's headlines announced that several people had drowned, and a few bodies had washed up on the beach near our hotel.

Ten days after returning home, our newspapers revealed the horrors of a devastating earthquake in Mexico City. We were lucky once again to have missed tragedy, but we weren't about to press our luck "south of the border" anytime soon.

"Air-conditioning" had real meaning in Africa ...
Botswana, 1992

Unless you're staying in lodges with built-in air-conditioning, you're pretty much on your own, when it comes to finding a way to cool down in the afternoon's incredible heat.

It was siesta time after lunch, but the 104-degree temperature in Chobe Park made resting in our hot canvas tent impossible. "Let's go to the dining tent and play solitaire," Shirley suggested, "at least we might get a breeze from the cross-ventilation." So, packing up our decks of cards, we headed through the quiet camp to the dining tent.

"At least there's a breeze, even if it is a hot one," I remarked. "Hey, I have an idea! Why don't we put on our heaviest twill shorts, and take a shower with our clothes on! That way, it will take awhile for the water to dry our clothes in the breeze, and we should stay cooler longer." A short time later, we were taking turns in the outdoor shower, drenching ourselves from head to toe, like two naughty children, before returning to the dining tent.

"That's more like it, I feel cooler already," I remarked.

"Good idea, but now the breeze is blowing our cards around," Shirley said, as she tried to catch the cards before they were whisked outside the tent. Then the tent's flaps started to blow furiously in the wind, and we peered outside, to see what was going on.

"Look at that!" I pointed across the dry, dusty plains. "It looks like a dust-devil." Surely it was, just as we'd seen in Kenya's Amboseli Park. It was like a mini tornado, just a whirl of dust. "It looks like it's heading our way," I commented in amazement. Like two morons, we continued to watch the approaching swirl of dust, sand, and earth. "It's heading straight for us, we'd better get out of here!" We picked up our cards, and kept a watchful eye. Suddenly, it veered to our left. "It's heading for Margie's tent!" I shouted. The words had barely left my mouth, and the whirling dust-devil picked up her tent, twirled it around, and dumped it upside down on some bushes, before veering off in another direction.

"Wow! That was a close one," Shirley mumbled in enough disbelief for both of us.

~ FAST FORWARD ~

Who needs a sauna to help lose weight— evaporate it away!
The Caprivi Strip, Namibia, 2003

When it's cold at home, a hot, sunny vacation destination sounds like the remedy. Best advice ... think twice!

Everyone knows about our winters in the Midwest—cold, gray, sometimes rainy, and always dull. That's usually when I drag out the colorful tour brochures, and see beautiful vacation spots in hot, sunny locations. The sky is so blue, and if there are palm trees, that's even better. You tend to forget how hot it can be, when there's snow on the ground. But when you get to that place, it's usually another matter.

Sure, we'd experienced the heat before—over one hundred in Myanmar and Botswana. But this time, we expected weather in the nineties, not over a hundred.

"How hot is it today?" I asked our guide.

He walked to the thermometer on the wall of the lodge. "Looks like it's about a hundred and twenty today," he responded nonchalantly.

"A *hundred and twenty*?" I shouted in horror. "Is it always like this?"

"Well, it's been hovering around that for the last few days," he answered.

Shirley and I followed the sandy path to our cabin, keeping our heads down in the brilliant sunlight. We couldn't get inside fast enough.

"I can't believe this heat!" I said turning to her.

She reached for her nightshirt, "I'm going to wet this down before putting it on, so it keeps me cool."

"Now that's a good idea. Maybe soaking in the shower, and not drying off would also help."

I emerged from the bathroom, body and nightshirt dripping from head to toe. I reached for a wicker chair, and put my feet up on the edge of the bed, placing a wet cloth over my face. Ten minutes later, I was dry as a bone. There wasn't even the hint of a breeze.

"My god," I whined, "I feel like I'm evaporating!"

SHE HUFFED AND SHE PUFFED, AND SHE BLEW THE PLANTS DOWN ...
HONG KONG 1993

In the city, many apartment dwellers are prone to keeping large potted plants on their small, small balconies—just to have some greenery around. They must have been surprised to find their plants lying in the middle of the sidewalk below, surrounded by pieces of the broken pots.

As anyone who's ever been to Hong Kong knows, its streets are filled morning, noon, and night with people. Neon lights shout the names of restaurants, stores, and hotels. Maybe that's why we became suspicious the morning after our arrival, when we opened the drapes and found the sidewalks and streets nearly bare. NO—not in Hong Kong! We took a closer look, and noticed that the bamboo scaffolding on a building across the street was dangling in the wind. Where were the cars, the buses, *any* traffic at all? We turned on CNN. "Typhoon Becky hit Hong Kong during the night," the broadcaster said, "electricity is off in some parts of the city, public transportation has ceased, and everyone is urged to stay home." What? This couldn't be—stay home?

We were worried that hours later, when our parents woke up, they'd be alarmed to hear there was a typhoon in Hong Kong, so we waited until a reasonable hour back home to call and tell them we were safe.

"Hello, mom!" Shirley shouted into the receiver. "We're in Hong Kong, and ..."

"Shirley! Bud, the girls are in Hong Kong," her mother called to her dad. "Thank goodness you weren't at those temples when the terrorists struck yesterday, killing all those poor tourists."

"Mom, that was in Luxor, Egypt—we're in *Hong Kong*—Egypt wasn't even on our itinerary."

"Well, then you're safe, dear."

"Well, yes, and no. We wanted to let you know that there was a typhoon here last night, but that everything is okay, and we're fine."

"It's nice to know you're having a good time. We haven't heard anything about a typhoon."

Suffice it to say that even our own parents probably hadn't looked at our itinerary; they just knew we were somewhere on the other side of the world. Finally, the weather had settled down, so we decided to take a walk to assess the damage. Fortunately, the typhoon hit late at night, so pedestrian traffic was probably pretty light when the potted plants on the balconies took a dive for the sidewalks below. We never did hear any sirens, or see any ambulances, so those were good signs.

We walked for blocks, until we found our way down to the waterfront's Ocean Terminal shopping arcade. The city was like a ghost town. Few people were on the streets, even though the rain had stopped hours before. The winds had died down, and the only things that hampered our leisurely stroll were those damn potted plants scattered all over the sidewalks. There were few places we could go, or little we could do. Almost everything was closed up from the night before, and people couldn't get to work without any public transportation.

Somehow, someone managed to get to work—the movie theatre was open. Did we really want to spend our time watching *Jurassic Park*? On the other hand, we didn't have any other options. We stepped to the ticket window.

"Where would you like to sit?" the young lady asked.

"Sit?" we asked in unison.

"Yes, we have assigned seating. Where would you like to sit?"

We selected two seats, and made our way inside. The usher showed us to our seats. The entire situation was more ridiculous than we even imagined at first, because we were the only people in the whole theatre! When we surfaced a few hours later, some neon signs were on above the stores and hotels, and traffic was beginning to operate once more—who would ever think we'd be glad to see traffic.

After such anticipation of returning to Hong Kong, this wasn't what we'd expected, but it was certainly one visit we'd never forget.

SO, WHAT'S A LITTLE BIT OF RAIN?
JAKARTA, INDONESIA

So, you're in the tropics ... it rains hard, and then it's over right? Wrong!

My plane circled Jakarta, and I glanced out of the window. The brown water surrounded the houses on stilts. I'd never seen a place where the rice fields came so close to the city. As usual, my guide was waiting for me as I exited the international arrival terminal. With a big smile, she introduced herself as Pat, and welcomed me. Then she said rather apologetically, "It's been raining." What else is new? It rained in Bali and threatened rain in Jogjakarta.

"What's a little bit of rain," I commented, trying to let her think I was ready to cope with anything.

"Yes, but it's been raining for over three days!" Well, now that was a different story. "And," she added, "the streets are all flooded."

"You mean those weren't rice fields I saw as we landed?" I asked in surprise.

"Oh no! Those are the flooded areas, and I'm not sure how much sightseeing we can do."

The driver pulled up to the curb with our van, and I wondered why he placed my luggage on the seat beside me, when the back floor of the van was empty. We left the airport, and started driving towards the city. Pat wasn't kidding about flooding! People were well above their knees in water (but you have to remember, they're very short people, so their knees were much closer to the ground than mine). Nonetheless, when the water started to slosh inside the door of the van, it began to get my attention—no wonder my luggage was sitting on the seat.

My eyes were open wide, as I looked all around me. Everywhere I could see, cars were stalled—many of them were Mercedes. We kept chugging along. More cars stalled, and people all around us were wading through the water—but I was safe inside the van—and we kept chugging along. Then some young men jumped on the back bumper, and our chugging van started to stammer. The driver shooed them away, and we chugged along. There were still more stalled cars, and then I started to give serious thought to the situation. What if *we* got stalled? We'd be stranded between the city and the airport, and no one could come out to help, because everyone else was in the same predicament.

Somehow, we managed to make it all the way into the city. Although there wasn't any more rain the following day, sightseeing was restricted, because of flooded streets. Jakarta was totally different from Jogjakarta—it was much more modern, and resembled Singapore with its glitzy hotels and office buildings. On the other hand, Jogjakarta had a third-world flavor, and was much more fun to explore. Upon returning to my hotel, I found a note from the management, urging me to depart several hours earlier than my flight time the next day, because many of the roads were still flooded.

The following morning, I concluded that if we should have a problem getting to the airport, so would everyone else on that flight—including the crew. Though it was a long, slow drive, we managed to keep a steady pace, and didn't encounter many flooded areas. As my good fortune continued, I arrived at the airport in plenty of time. Better yet, even the crew was there!

Pay Attention to Those Weather Reports ...
Yangtze River, China, 2000

Two days into our cruise on the mighty Yangtze River, and I suddenly recalled a short article I'd read the previous spring, buried amidst the newspaper's many advertisements, so I almost missed it. Now it was now early July, but the words haunted me, "heavy rains in the northern provinces of China have led to flooding along the Yangtze River." Little did I know at the time, that I'd find myself cruising the river that summer—and never could I have guessed that the flooding would have such an impact on my journey many months later.

The day started as usual, with lots of sunshine, extreme temperatures, and high humidity. Our small ship was winding its way through the gorges without a problem. The brown waters of the Yangtze were rapidly flowing around us, and cigarette butts and paper coffee cups were swirling past the ship. We were becoming accustomed to seeing this sort of trash in the river (probably washed down from the mountainside villages), but a dead dog and, yes, even a dead man's body, didn't go unnoticed. They were more proof that the river could be an unforgiving enemy. Old buildings and small farms dotted the mountainsides above us. Occasionally, a historic temple would beckon the photographers to the side of the ship for a picture to verify its existence, before either being relocated or lost to the depths of the rising river—a sad result of the dam project.

About halfway through our cruise, it became obvious that we were at a standstill—literally! The captain came over the loud speaker, informing us that due to the high level of the water, it would not be possible for us to take an excursion through the lesser gorges. We spent about a day-and-a-half in port, waiting for a decision about the continuation of our cruise. It was too dangerous to open the locks that would allow us to proceed to our destination, because of the high water level, and it seemed like the captain was making announcements about sailing conditions every hour over the loud speaker.

Judging from the reactions of the passengers, one would have thought we were stranded in outer space. I tried to put the fears of the people in my group to rest, by reminding them that the ship was in communication with their office and the various tour operators, so it wasn't as though no one knew where we were. But that didn't work.

Every time we heard the loudspeaker system turn on for another broadcast from the captain, our hearts sank lower and lower. No news had been good news. We couldn't move ahead, and we were losing precious vacation time. Would we ever make up the time, and see the other sights in Xian and Beijing that were on our itinerary?

Finally ... the word we were waiting for! The captain announced that there was another ship coming downstream. The passengers from that ship would be transferred by bus to our ship; and we would be transferred to theirs. Good game plan—but the transfer was to take place late at night, when the other ship arrived on their side of the locks. To make matters worse, it was a ninety-minute ride from port on a winding road through the mountains, to the other ship.

Thirty-five ... forty-five ... fifty-five ... I counted the steps down to the ship. There were many ... it was very dark ... we were grasping our carry-on luggage ... there weren't any handrails ... and it was raining—hard! At last, we made it aboard our new ship, and could continue our cruise.

The ship couldn't move any faster, and the time was slipping away all too quickly. Would we have time to see the Terra Cotta Warriors in Xian? We'd lost the entire day, and were to fly out of Xian in the morning. To our surprise, the museum housing the stone warriors was going to reopen for us. But the drive from the airport was at least an hour long, and we wouldn't arrive until around midnight. Surprise again, we were given the royal treatment. Not only was the museum open, but we were also allowed to film the stone warriors—something strongly prohibited thirteen years before. In addition, we were treated to a movie about the creation, demise, and discovery of the warriors in a 360-degree theater. And to top off the evening, the farmer who made the historic discovery was available to autograph books, postcards, whatever we wanted—for five dollars each.

The pace had certainly picked up, but we were still about a day behind. The government tourist office bumped local passengers from a flight, so we could continue to Beijing. Two days' activities were squeezed into one, as we visited the Forbidden City, climbed the Great Wall, walked around the Summer Palace, and cruised its lake, before ending up at the Temple of Heaven. We concluded our whirlwind tour of Beijing by dropping into our beds—exhausted!

Chapter 7

Oh Those Men

**From Ecuador to Egypt, Hong Kong to Croatia, and everywhere in between.
As though the jetlag, strange food, and weather aren't enough to deal with ...**

Hilton Hotel (Mexico City 1969) ... "Excuse me, Senorita, but you have a telephone call." I looked at the waiter, and wondered who would be calling me in Mexico. Hesitating, I picked up the phone. "Hello?" "Senorita, I watched you walk through the dining room, and would like to meet you ..."

Da Ciccerauchio Restaurant (Rome 1970) ... The waiter presented me with a business card that read, "To the lady in the black dress, I like to meet you for a drink, please come to the lobby." Was someone watching me? A strange feeling came over me, as I looked around the outdoor patio at the other tables, wondering which lone man had sent the card ...

Victoria Falls Hotel (Victoria Falls, Rhodesia 1974) ... Geri and I were enjoying the afternoon siesta, when the phone rang. I answered it, and the voice on the other end asked, "Are you the girl with the ginger-colored hair?" "Who *is* this?" "I was the pilot on your flight over the falls this morning. I'm just calling to see if you want to go to a party tonight."

Need I say more? You know the sort ... but you never know when or where you'll meet one who will make a lasting impression. I have lots of lasting impressions—some I wish I'd even forget!

Shame on you, if you jumped ahead to read this chapter!

It pays to dream big, because sometimes dreams really do come true!
Bogota, Colombia, 1973

When I was a little girl, I loved a picture my aunt and uncle had in their basement. It was of a beautiful Spanish dancer, whose flowing dress was made of brightly colored satin ribbons. My cousin and I used to listen to old records in the basement, as we pretended to be that beautiful lady in the picture, and danced to my favorite song, "Lady of Spain." Couple all that with a vivid imagination, and my trip to South America was about to be a dream come true.

Names of cities like Rio de Janeiro and Buenos Aires intrigued me from childhood. But the Latin music and dance also fascinated me ... sambas, rumbas, tangos. I dreamed of dancing to the Latin beats with some handsome man, like in the old movies. But that wasn't likely to happen—I was lucky I could get a foxtrot out of someone.

Geri and I were settling into our airplane seats in Miami, when I looked at the passengers still boarding—and directly into the dark eyes of a gorgeous man. Stopping briefly in the aisle in front of our seats, he stared straight into my eyes, smiled, and nodded at me, as he passed. Another man, who did the same, followed him. As they continued down the aisle, Geri and I turned our heads to see where they were sitting.

Throughout the flight, we kept glancing at the two strangers like a couple of schoolgirls, only to be met with glances of equal interest. The flirtation continued for what seemed like a very short flight to South America. Before the announcement came to prepare for landing, I dashed to the lavatory. The object of my attention was returning to his seat, and smiled as he passed by. On the way to my seat, he put his arm out to stop me.

"Where are you going?" he asked, just as the flight attendant told everyone to take their seat for landing. "That's all right," he said, "I'll find you at the airport." And find me he did. "Where are you staying?" he asked, when he saw me at the baggage carousel.

"We're at the Tequendama Hotel."

"I'll see you there, we must be on our way," and before I knew what happened, the two strangers were leaving the airport.

Our tour guide passed out the room keys at the hotel, and I still hadn't seen the two men from the plane. I was very disappointed, but when I turned around, they were walking across the lobby towards us.

"Hello again, my name is Esvaldo, and this is my brother, Ricardo. How long will you be here?" he asked.

When we told him we were in Bogota for only a couple days, he suggested that we meet later that evening, after we were settled in. The time couldn't pass fast enough, until we met again.

"There's a dance in the ballroom. Shall we see what's going on?" Esvaldo asked.

Before I knew "what was going on," he was twirling me around the dance floor like he was Fred Astair and I was Ginger Rogers. Then the beat of the music changed, and the percussions took over. Esvaldo raised his arms over his head, snapping his fingers, while he looked at me with those beautiful black eyes. He moved his shoulders and hips to the rhythm of the Latin music, and I knew that this was the moment I had waited for since I was a little girl—this was my dream come true. His sensuous movements drew me in and, before I knew it, I was following him as though we'd been dance partners all our lives. When the song ended, I asked him the name of the dance. "It's called the cumbia—you like it?" It was definitely like something you'd see only in the movies!

I couldn't sleep a wink that night, and the following morning at breakfast, I couldn't stop swaying in my chair to the rhythms of the cumbia, still resonating in my head. That evening, Geri and I were having a drink at the hotel's rooftop nightclub. Just as were leaving, Esvaldo entered the room and walked over to our table.

"Are you leaving so soon?" He asked in disappointment.

"It's so noisy in here."

"Would you like to go dancing at some place more quiet?"

"Well ..." I hesitated.

"Come on, I'll get you home in time for your flight tomorrow morning," he said, taking my hand. I waited for Geri to stop me, but all she could say was, "I'll leave the door unlocked."

Entering the discotheque, I first noticed the frosted glass dance floor, lit from below by brightly colored lights. The room could have been filled with people, or it may have been empty, I don't really know, because as far as I was concerned, we were the only two people dancing.

I DREAMED OF FERNANDO LAMAS, BUT FOUND MYSELF IN THE ARMS OF ... PEPE?*
QUITO, ECUADOR, 1973

(*In 1973, Fernando Lamas—you know, Lorenzo's dad—was the equivalent of Antonio Banderas)

Just my good fortune, a slow song with a man whose head barely reached my ample chest! What a sight we must have been—he swayed left, and I swayed right.

Geri stared at me with puppy-dog eyes, and I couldn't resist. I'd be selfish.

"Pepe really wants to go out with you tonight," she pleaded on his behalf.

"Okay, okay, I'll do it, but only so you won't feel guilty leaving me alone while you go out with Paul (our tour guide)." I agreed to go to the hotel's discotheque that evening with Pepe, our local guide, but only because it would be a safe place, with lots of people around.

When we entered the dark discotheque, it took awhile for my eyes to adjust before I noticed how empty it was. Geri and Paul were romantically tucked away in a booth, and obviously engrossed in conversation, because neither acknowledged my wave, as I brushed right past their table.

Pepe led me to the other side of the room. I sat down on one of the many couches, and he sat next to me, sliding his arm around me. Without giving him much of a chance to settle in too comfortably, I asked if we might dance (goodness knows, there was room to spare on the brass dance floor). Reluctantly, he followed me to the center of the floor. To my dismay, the music changed from a rock beat to a slow song, and Pepe once again slid not one, but both arms around me! It was then that I noticed how much shorter he was.

Finally, the song ended, and I headed back to the couch, with Pepe traipsing behind me. Perhaps I could keep him engaged in a conversation, since he spoke fluent English. It was customary in discotheques at the time to project films on various subject matters on a large screen. Tonight's feature was a bullfight, a sport I had seen performed, and found of interest. I began to question Pepe, who was encouraged to see me interested in something (he probably thought it was him). He leaned closer and closer, explaining every aspect of bullfighting, from how the bulls are raised and prepared for the bullring, to how the matador must learn all he can about the bull's personality and weaknesses within the first few minutes of their encounter. He was very enthusiastic, and continued to lean still closer. Then I got my first sniff of Pepe's breath—ugh! He leaned forward, and I leaned back.

In the '70s vinyl was not solely used to make records, it played a very important part in our wardrobes. We had vinyl boots, hats, coats—and I even had a white vinyl dress. It looked like leather, but smelled like my mother's kitchen tablecloth. I happened to be wearing it that evening, and I guess we were somewhat well matched—Pepe and I—he with his bad breath, and me with my smelly dress.

The long zipper down the front of my dress had more than one convenience. Pepe began demonstrating some of the matador's passes. When he wasn't looking, I slid the zipper down a little, so I could get a whiff of the oilcloth fumes, as I slouched in my seat. I could nestle my nose inside the v-neck for a scent that was as welcome as a bouquet of flowers by now.

Somehow, I survived, and thanked Pepe for the "interesting" evening. Geri was waiting up for me.

"Did you and Pepe go to the discotheque? Paul and I didn't see you there!"

A PERFECT VACATION, A PERFECT DINNER, A PERFECT MAN (WELL, TWO OUT OF THREE ISN'T BAD)!
HONG KONG 1975

So, by now you've figured out that I'm an incurable romantic. Maybe someday I'll learn my lesson.

Hong Kong was exciting and beautiful. Whenever I entered our room at the Hilton, I exclaimed to Geri that the view was more breathtaking than before—then, I'd reach for my camera, trying one more time to film the wide-sailed Chinese junks drifting across the bay from the mainland. Our first trip to Asia was winding down, and we selected one of the hotel's finer restaurants for our last dinner. We donned our long dresses one more time, and entered the Victorian-styled dining room, where the maitre'd seated us at a table in the center of the room. Then I noticed the music—my *favorite* music—LATIN music (in Hong Kong?). I swayed to *Besame Mucho, Brazil, Sabor Ami, and Perfidia*. I was in heaven. Then my attention was drawn to the pianist, and he noticed me—noticing him! Our eyes locked, and I'm sure I blushed, but then again, it could have been the reflection from the crimson-flocked wallpaper. It was as though he was playing only for me, because everyone else in the room seemed to disappear. Looking at him more intently, I guessed him to be Italian.

By the time my duck dinner arrived, I'd forgotten about eating. Geri's back was to the pianist, so I gave her all the details about him, and how he was returning my glances. Then I realized that I had a small problem ... I couldn't eat my duck while his eyes were locked on me. "Geri, I want to take a bite of my duck, do you think you could move a little to the right, so he doesn't see me?" I felt like a movie director, between giving her play-by-play descriptions of the glances I was receiving, and telling her to sway a little to the left, bend to the right, sit up straight. Somehow, I managed to finish my meal without the pianist seeing me drop my peas, or wipe the orange sauce from my chin. It was time for his break, and I just knew he'd make his way to our table.

"Oh, Geri, what shall I say? He's so attractive, and his music is so beautiful." I knew everything was too perfect, so I grasped at anything just to burst my own bubble. "What if he's really short?"

Precisely as I predicted, the musician made his way from table to table, until he was right in front of me. "Are you enjoying the music?" he asked, as he looked at me with a grin.

"Very much. Latin music is my favorite."

"Where are you from?" he inquired, in a thick Italian accent. Was this too perfect!

"We're from the States—the Chicago area."

"I hope you've enjoyed your stay in Hong Kong?"

Before he could say another word, I could hear a loud pop in my head, as my bubble was bursting—no, make that exploding! I realized that he was looking at me nearly eye level, and I was sitting down. I didn't hear another word he had to say, and I only hoped that my responses were appropriate. Eventually, he walked back to his piano. As we left the dining room, I smiled weakly and waved. Once again, my heart sank. I knew no one could be that perfect—but I couldn't deny that his music was wonderful.

Pursued like an Egyptian princess (hairy arms and all) ...
Egypt 1976

All this attention ... what would it have been like for a real beauty?

The young bellman deposited my carry-on bag inside my room at Cairo's Meridien Hotel, and then he just stood there looking at me, as he closed his fingers over his tip.

"Is there something else?" I asked curiously.

"You have hair on your arms!" He blurted out. Aghast, I didn't know what to say. I was in total disbelief.

"Don't Egyptian women have hair on their arms?"

"No," he retorted, still delighted with his discovery. Perhaps I should have known better, but I was still curious, and pressed on.

"Do you like it?" I asked, a little embarrassed at the thought that I might be encouraging this conversation. He perked up, his eyes twinkled, and he answered in the affirmative. I knew right then and there that I had to get him out of my room, and fast!

The following day, the more adventurous in our group climbed the great pyramid of Cheops—from the inside. The wooden ramp was very steep and narrow. I grasped the handrails, cameras dangling from each wrist. We finally reached a platform that provided the opportunity to stand up from our crouched position. An elderly woman in the group began to cough, and couldn't catch her breath. Our Egyptian guide lifted his djalaba, exposing his skinny, dried up old legs protruding from his knee-length boxer shorts. He began fanning her, but the flurry of activity stirred the dust all the more. When her coughing spell subsided, we proceeded with our climb. I grasped the handrails of the metal ladder firmly, when suddenly, I felt hands on my buttocks pushing me up—they belonged to our guide, who stood below me, revealing a nearly toothless smile.

At last, we reached the king's room. I raised my head, and was stricken with utter disappointment. The room and sarcophagus were void of any painting, decorations, or additional furnishings and artifacts. Fluorescent lights overhead only accentuated the dark, drab room.

The climb down was perhaps even more challenging, because we had to remain bent over as we descended the narrow wooden ramp. Finally, I could see light ahead. I approached the door, and the guide patted my behind again, as he stretched his dirty palm out for a tip. "That pat *was* your tip," I spat in anger, as I rushed past him. Only two days into the trip, and my impression of the native men was dwindling faster than a bottle of ice water on a hot day!

Luxor was the next stop on our itinerary. Eight of us in the tour group were dining at a round table one night at the New Winter Palace Hotel. Afterwards, the waiter presented each of us with the bill for our drinks. As he handed mine to me, he asked for the room number. Assuming that he needed it for the check, I gave it to him. Leaning over, he whispered, "Single or double bed?" I was aghast at his forwardness, but it was about to end, as I angrily blurted out, "Yes, I have a *double* bed!" so everyone at my table could hear. This time, it was the waiter who was in shock, as he disappeared into the woodwork.

The next day, I found myself eyeing a necklace in the window of one of the jewelry stores in an arcade. Stepping inside, I asked the young man at the counter if I might see the colorful "mummy bead" necklace in the window. "We have them upstairs," he said, as he directed me to the narrow staircase. There was no one else in the small store, and I hesitated, but he led the way with apparent disinterest, so I followed him. He opened the cabinet containing the jewelry and removed the necklace from its box. Moving closely behind me, he tried to fasten it. Before he could finish, I pushed myself away and ran down the stairs muttering that I had changed my mind, as I slammed the glass door.

GO FOR IT THE FIRST TIME AROUND...
SPLIT, CROATIA, 1978

We don't often get a chance for an encore, so maybe we should make wiser choices the first time around. Then again, maybe our first choice was the wise one.

Standing in the lobby of our hotel in Split, our young tour guide Yolanda warned us, "One more thing, all the men in Split think they are Don JOO-wans" (she did mean "Don Juans," didn't she?). No sooner had she closed her mouth, than a bellman—the first "Don" appeared. He was mouth-watering—very tall, with dark hair and blue eyes! He grabbed my suitcase, and headed towards the elevator, which already had a crowd blocking the doors.

"Never mind," he said, "we take the service elevator—follow me." Before I could protest, he dashed off with my luggage, as I trailed behind. By this time, my head cold was wearing me out, and I just wanted to get to my room for a nap. I followed him into the elevator, and the door closed slowly, locking the two of us inside. The elevator began creeping upwards with some hesitation. I was concerned that it might get stuck, but apparently, he didn't mind at all. Before I knew it, he turned around and stepped towards me, pressing my back against the wall. Placing a hand on each of my shoulders, he leaned down and planted a wonderful kiss on my lips. Thank goodness he didn't let go of me when the kiss ended, because by this time, my knees were so weak I thought I'd faint. I didn't know if I was weak from the cold or his kiss, but it was probably a combination of both. Apparently, the shock on my face gave me away. Looking down at me and deeply into my eyes, he whispered, "Don't worry, little one, I won't hurt you. You don't have to be afraid." "Little one?" I don't think *anyone* ever called me "little one," except perhaps the doctor in the delivery room, when he presented me to my parents the day I was born. What a welcome to Split—this sure beat a flower lei presented by hula dancers in Hawaii!

At last, the elevator reached my floor. Because I was traveling as a single on this tour, I usually ended up with a room smaller than my closet at home; and it was generally located in the hidden corners of the hotels. This room was no exception. Somehow, I managed to find the strength to move one foot in front of the other, and follow Don down the dreary corridor to the hidden room tucked away in the bowels of the building. I was very apprehensive.

As I anticipated, the room was so small that I could hardly stretch my arms out on either side of me without touching both walls. What a good excuse for me to wait in the hallway, while he placed my luggage inside, where there was barely space for one person *and* the luggage, much less two people.

He turned to me, "I'll be through working at seven-thirty. If you'd like to go out, meet me in the lobby." Before I knew it, he was off like the bura winds of Croatia. The offer was soooooo tempting. Following dinner, I kept glancing at the hands on my watch, as I peeked through the slats of the banister that overlooked the lobby below. It was seven twenty-five. I still had five minutes to dash down the stairs to meet him. Seven twenty-nine. It was almost time—I had butterflies in my stomach. Finally, it was seven-thirty. He appeared in the lobby downstairs. "No, you can't even consider meeting him," I told myself. I knew I was using my cold as an excuse, coupled with the fact that I needed to recover for my long trip home. "But ..." No, I was right, I couldn't go. I could see him in the lobby, looking around—probably pretty confident that I'd be there. I suddenly felt a whole lot stronger.

~ FAST FORWARD ~

THE SECOND TIME IS NEVER AS GOOD!
SPLIT, CROATIA, 2004

As I anticipated revisiting this enchanting ancient city on the Dalmatian Coast, my mind wandered back to my brief elevator encounter many years before.

The war with Serbia had taken its toll, and I wondered if the hotel I stayed in twenty-six years earlier was still standing. Many hotels had been used by the Croatian government to house refugees during the war, which ended ten years earlier. As a result, they needed major renovations. Our hotel was a prime example. I looked at the hotel list the tour company had provided, but only one name sounded familiar, and it wasn't *this* one.

As I climbed the winding staircase to the dining room on the mezzanine level, a strange feeling came over me. Glancing over my shoulder, I didn't recognize anything about the lobby. The registration desk was very large, and the area behind it led to a few shops. No, this wasn't the same hotel, was it? When I left the dining room, my eyes caught the banister surrounding the staircase. I peeked between the wooden slats, and I could see the lobby. I remembered peeking through the slats to see "Don Joo-wan". It *was* the same hotel! Yes, I recalled that it was located on the waterfront. I described my recollection of the previous hotel to our tour guide, and he confirmed that the hotel had undergone renovation, and that the section we were staying in had been added after the war.

From that moment on, I looked at every man working in the hotel very curiously. Could there be a slim chance that Don had gotten caught in the war, and his life stood still? After all these years, might he still be working there—perhaps in another capacity? But all the men were much too old.

I retired that evening, with visions of Don still swirling in my head, then the swirls turned to my stomach. I quickly realized that all this swirling was churning up my dinner, and dashed to the bathroom. A good portion of the remainder of the night was spent with my arms around the toilet bowel, as my dinner made an encore performance. Despite feeling like I'd been run over by a bus, I couldn't help but laugh. Twenty-six years earlier, I could have had my arms around a real Don Juan. Now I was clutching a porcelain bowl as though it was my dearest friend. Sometimes, you just have to go for a thing the first time around … the second time is never as good!

Too good to be true ...
Mombasa, Kenya, 1988

It was a setting right out of a movie ... exotic location, beautiful hotel. But one thing was missing ...

The warm evening breeze from the Indian Ocean floated through the French doors of the thatch-roofed dining room. The candles on the white tablecloths flickered, and the fragrance of the bougainvilleas on the veranda drifted throughout the room. Caught up in the romance of the Moorish-styled Serena Beach Hotel, I ignored the conversations going on around me, and allowed my imagination to wander. The setting was perfect. Well, almost perfect—there was one thing missing—an attractive man. Who would fit into this sophisticated, romantic setting? I thought and thought, but not too long, when I found the perfect man. No sooner had his name come to mind, than I found him sitting at the table in front of me.

It couldn't be, could it? Was that really Sean Connery? I nudged the friend next to me, and asked her to sneak a look. She had to agree that there was definitely a resemblance. We mentioned this to a few other people in our party, who concurred. I couldn't stop staring—why, even the woman he was with resembled Sean Connery's wife—this was *too* coincidental. I asked the maitre'd if he knew the name of the man at the table across from me.

"Do you think that could be the actor Sean Connery?"

"It could be, madam, but I'm not sure," he answered. "Although I know that he is to visit the hotel to make an advertisement."

That did it ... I *knew* it was Sean Connery! Eventually, the couple left the dining room, and moved to another area for coffee. Now I was confronted with a serious problem. Earlier in the day, I had a nasty altercation with a rough wave on the beach, which resulted in a badly swollen knee. After burying it beneath ice for hours, I could hardly limp, let alone climb the many stairs leading to the lounge, where the mysterious couple retired for after-dinner coffee. With a little enticing (and a pathetic look on my face), one of the men in our party took pity on me, and agreed to make a trip to the lounge for a better look in a brightly lit room. When he returned a short time later, he pronounced the man "a good look-a-like, but *no* Sean Connery." What do men know! I should have sent women on that mission. I was convinced that if I could hear the mystery man speak, I'd know immediately if he was Sean Connery. I suddenly remembered that I'd brought a small tape recorder to dinner with me, so I could tape the music on the patio later that evening.

Retreating to the poolside, I realized that Sean and the Missus were standing next to some bushes on the other side of a curved three-foot brick wall that surrounded the foliage. Perfect! How lucky could I get? I sat myself around the bend on the wall, not at all conspicuous in my hot pink gauze harem pants. As though that wasn't bad enough, I stretched my arm around the bushes, holding a tape recorder in the palm of my hand. Frustration set in, because there was too much background noise and my tape recorder couldn't pick up their voices. Disappointed, I hobbled away to a chair at the edge of the patio, a broken woman.

A little while later, the band started playing and couples walked over to the patio to dance. Peering through the darkness, I recognized the white dinner jacket—it was Sean and the Missus! I watched, and watched, and watched. Missus swayed left to the music, Sean jerked to the right. "What's going on?" I asked myself. Sean acted like he had two left feet! This couldn't be the same man who danced so gracefully through James Bond movies, and a host of others.

The following morning at breakfast, various people in my party asked if I was still convinced that I'd seen Sean Connery the previous night.

"That wasn't Sean Connery," I answered with great conviction.

"How do you know? What made you change your mind?"

"That guy had two left feet—didn't you see him dance? It *couldn't* have been Sean Connery!"

ON A SCALE OF ONE TO TEN, "RANGOON" WAS AN ELEVEN!
YANGON (RANGOON), MYANMAR, 1993

The city was in a near state of decay. The hotel was worn out and tired looking, but "Rangoon" turned out to be a diamond in the rough.

The dining room was crowded at the Inya Lake Hotel in Yangon, formerly known as Rangoon, and Bill, Shirley, and I were the only Westerners there. Waiters squeezed between the tables of the crowded room, balancing trays of rice on their shoulders, like snow-white mountains.

Loud, hectic, colorful, busy. No one and nothing seemed to stand out. The room was just a mass of sounds, smells, and noise. Until, that is, I glanced beyond Bill's shoulder, and spotted "him." My mouth fell open, my eyes grew larger, and a big smile spread across my face. For there at a table across the crowded room, sat a man whose movie-star good looks had me mesmerized. Apparently, my pleasure was all too obvious, because he looked squarely at me and smiled.

Bill stopped talking to ask why my face was so flushed. Ignoring him, I turned to Shirley.

"Did you see what's sitting over there?"

"Uh huuuuuh," she responded with equal pleasure.

"What?" Bill asked, wondering why he lost his audience.

"Only one of the finest specimens I've ever seen!" I retorted, still keeping my eyes glued to the stranger. Despite my pleas not to turn around, Bill's head almost spun off his neck, as he turned it backwards to catch a glimpse.

"What's your name?" Bill teased, as if asking the stranger.

"Rangoon—Johnny Rangoon!" Bill answered himself.

From that day on, whenever Shirley and I rate men, it's always on the "Johnny Rangoon" comparison scale. Who'd have thought I would need to travel half way around the world to find a man who ranked eleven on a scale of ten!

About the Author

The author has traveled abroad annually for more than thirty years, visiting over ninety countries on six continents. Her initial goal was to have traveled around the world by the age of thirty; but by that time, international travel had become an addiction and a lifestyle.

She works for a medical society that brings her into contact with people from all over the globe. Knowing about their homelands has made their interaction a rich and rewarding experience for everyone.

When not working or traveling, the author resides in Darien, Illinois, a suburb southwest of Chicago.

978-0-595-41754-4
0-595-41754-X

Printed in the United States
96999LV00004B/172/A